MW01032300

A City Laid Waste

A CITY LAID WASTE

THE CAPTURE, SACK, AND DESTRUCTION OF THE CITY OF COLUMBIA

WILLIAM GILMORE SIMMS

EDITED WITH AN INTRODUCTION BY DAVID AIKEN

University of South Carolina Press

© 2005 University of South Carolina

Published in Columbia, South Carolina,
by the University of South Carolina Press

Manufactured in the United States of America

09 08 07 06   5 4 3 2

Library of Congress Cataloging-in-Publication Data

Simms, William Gilmore, 1806–1870.
    A city laid waste : the capture, sack, and destruction of the city of Columbia /
William Gilmore Simms ; edited with an introduction by David Aiken.
        p. cm.
    Articles originally published in the Columbia Phoenix newspaper.
    Includes bibliographical references and index.
    ISBN 1-57003-596-2 (cloth : alk. paper)
    1. Columbia (S.C.)—History—Burning, 1865. 2. Columbia (S.C.)—
History—Burning, 1865—Personal narratives. 3. Sherman, William T.
(William Tecumseh), 1820–1891. I. Aiken, David, 1941– II. Title: Columbia
phoenix (Columbia, S.C. : Triweekly). III. Title.
    E477.75.S55 2005
    973.7'38'0975771—dc22

                                                                    2005013307

Dedicated to the good people of South Carolina,
whose representatives continue to meet in Columbia,
a city laid waste in 1865 only to rise from her ashes
with the renewed vigor and natural beauty we see
today in the restored State House

CONTENTS

ILLUSTRATIONS

ACKNOWLEDGMENTS

Knowing nothing about the spreading tendencies of mint, my wife poked a hole in the soil beside our front porch one spring day and patted into place a sprig of mint. In no time at all, two rivers of green were flowing—one on either side of our driveway from the front yard to the back. So it has been with my work on Simms. Intending to complete a single project, I would begin digging in libraries and used book stores. I would tuck a sprig of Simms's work into place only to find other projects sprouting up all around me: this particular project started out with what I took for a passing interest in Simms as a war poet. As it spread to encompass the editorial work Simms did for the *Columbia Phoenix*, I began to acquire debts of gratitude to people both on my right and on my left.

In the twelve years I have been lecturing on William Gilmore Simms throughout the Carolina Lowcountry, I have never been let down by the efficient staff of the South Caroliniana Library. If one staff member was unable to help me with a specific problem, she directed me to someone else who could. I am especially grateful to Allen Stokes, who found the lost copies of the *Columbia Phoenix*, and to Beth Bilderback for locating suitable illustrations for the present edition.

As a founding member and former president of the Simms Society, I have been privileged to associate with and to draw inspiration from the most dedicated Simms scholars and enthusiasts in the country. Becoming acquainted with Simms descendants at society gatherings and conventions has been memorable. These good people have displayed entertaining wit and an active willingness to supply source materials, financial support, and encouragement in the furtherance of Simms research. Anne Simms Pincus, a direct descendant of Simms's son Gilmore, has been particularly cheerful and supportive throughout the years, as also has been Mary Simms Furman and the whole Kello family. Contributors to the *Simms Review*, published twice a year by the society, are praiseworthy individuals who consistently submit quality articles, notes, and announcements pertinent to the life and writings of William Gilmore Simms. These gracious people have enhanced my own appreciation of Simms while increasing our knowledge of Simms's historical influence and his importance to scholars in this and other countries, some as far away as Russia and Japan.

The late A. J. Conyers, professor of theology at the George W. Truett Theological Seminary at Baylor University, was a special source of encouragement. He not only shared my appreciation for the Bible as literature but also admired, as I do, the subtle ways in which Simms employed his own knowledge of biblical literature when conveying messages of hope and faith throughout his writings, especially in those works he produced during and after the War between the States. Chip Conyers was the best example of a Christian scholar, not only in subject matter but also in spirit and character. While I mourn the recent loss of so good a friend, I remain grateful for the memory of his influence and example.

To my students whose genuine interest and thoughtful classroom questions motivated me to dig deeper into the life and works of Simms, I offer sincere thanks for the many nudges. To my former staff colleague Barbara Bruce McGee I am indebted. She undertook the tedious task of typing the original manuscript from microfilm. Kathleen Hilliard for a summer and Timothy Manning for half of a summer were my capable research assistants when I was the Visiting William Gilmore Simms Professor at the South Caroliniana Library in Columbia, sponsored by the Simms family. These assistants joined in the challenge of trying to decipher words that appeared almost illegible even when held under various magnifiers. By 2004 all but one word had been identified. No doubt inspired by a deep longing to rid our living room of the mountain of paperwork engendered by this project, my wife spent a month with several dictionaries, an assortment of magnifiers, and the tiny black spots representing the illusive letters that began that one little word. Identifying the appropriate word, which she finally found in the *Oxford English Dictionary*, and seeing it fit perfectly into its proper place brought about an understandable conclusion to my dear wife's patience. She reclaimed our living room, and I carried my materials to a back room now fondly referred to as "the dog house."

James Everett Kibler and Donald W. Livingston read the completed manuscript and provided helpful suggestions along with sincere appreciation. Alex Moore, acquisitions editor of the University of South Carolina Press, has stayed in touch via telephone and email, providing much pertinent information and timely assistance. Patient and understanding throughout the process, he has conveyed professional guidance in each stage of the project's transition from proposal to completion.

To my loving and supportive wife, Della Jean Aiken, I own a huge debt of gratitude. She has been living with Simms manuscripts and towers of books since my 1989 introduction to Simms's great novel *The Cassique of Kiawah*. Near the completion of each of my Simms projects, I invariably promise her there will be no more. Yet here I am, dozens of Simms publications down the line, ready to offer the same old assurances, when the image of spreading mint mysteriously comes to mind.

A NOTE ON THE TEXT

William Gilmore Simms's eyewitness account of the destruction of Columbia, written in the immediate aftermath of the conflagration and published serially in a small newspaper, the *Columbia Phoenix*, has never before been made available. Simms's report ran for ten consecutive issues, and even though it had no byline, people knew that Simms was the writer long before his authorship was declared in the 12 October 1865 issue. Very few copies of the *Columbia Phoenix* have survived. What follows is a transcription of the original serial account published in the *Columbia Phoenix*, vol. 1, nos. 1–10 (21 March–10 April 1865).

This serial publication includes "The Fire," a list of destroyed properties in addition to displaced owners and occupants, which ran in the first three issues. Except for the final installment, entitled "Conflagration of Columbia," sections were designated only with roman numerals, for a total of thirty-five. Section XV was republished in another newspaper, the *Daily Carolinian*, on 29 April 1865. The complete run of "The Capture, Sack, and Destruction of the City of Columbia" appeared on 21 March, 23 March, 25 March, 28 March, 30 March, 1 April, 4 April, 6 April, 8 April, and 10 April 1865.

Simms revised "The Capture, Sack, and Destruction of the City of Columbia" for a pamphlet edition, which was published at the end of 1865, after the Confederacy had fallen, changing the title to *Sack and Destruction of the City of Columbia, S.C.*. This pamphlet edition includes a few factual corrections, a very few stylistic emendations, and some changes of tone, in which Simms deleted some of his harsh rhetoric. Simms also made some structural changes in the pamphlet edition. Since he made these slight changes after the fall of the Confederacy, he was clearly responding to the newly imposed economic, cultural and political dependency of the South. The pamphlet edition of 1865 has been republished on several occasions, but the original serial account has not. This edition seeks to make that remarkable document available for the first time since 1865. The best discussion of the publication history of "The Capture, Sack, and Destruction" and of *Sack and Destruction* is by Nicholas Meriwether in the *Simms Review* 12 (Summer 2004): 25–37.

The serial account is important for the historical, cultural, and literary reasons discussed in the introduction.

A City Laid Waste

INTRODUCTION
War News

I.

On 20 February 1865 Sherman and his troops ended their four-day invasion of the capital of South Carolina. They left behind a city reduced to ashes and a trail of destruction that could not be described in any of the city's newspapers, simply because none of them had survived the onslaught. Newspaper offices and printing presses had all been destroyed. Paper—already a precious commodity in the war-torn South—was all but impossible to find. It seemed for a while as if any hope of publicizing the event had, like the city of Columbia, gone up in smoke. Fortunately, the city had a visitor who had arrived only days before Sherman's attack, a man who was rarely without hope for any extended period of time and who was in his element whenever he turned his attention to the business of creating a newspaper.

William Gilmore Simms, already an internationally known author, had seen and heard too much to sit in silence when there was a big story to be told. Within a month of the city's destruction, he and Julian A. Selby were united in taking on the challenge of producing a triweekly newspaper that would be called the *Columbia Phoenix*. Selby, owner of the burned-out *South Carolinian*, was a printer eager to begin publishing again as soon as possible. He needed the best editor available, someone with experience in rapidly producing quality material under pressure. The obvious choice was Simms, who agreed to become editor and who searched the ruins of the *Carolinian* office, locating a composing stick in which the first lines of the new paper could be set up for the sake of continuity and tradition. Although he was forced to travel great distances under trying circumstances, Selby succeeded in locating paper, press, and type for the venture.

In Selby's absence Simms set about the task of collecting eyewitness accounts to add to his own observations and experiences. He also made an extensive list of all property destroyed, noting the streets on which the property had been located, the persons to whom the property had belonged, the people living there when it was destroyed, and the contents of the buildings that had been lost in the fires. Simms likely returned to making his own ink and candles, skills he had mastered earlier in the war in order to pursue his craft when all writing supplies had dwindled.

The South Caroliniana Library in Columbia has a full collection of the trifolds edited by Simms and published in 1865 by Selby. Each newspaper is approximately six by eighteen inches, folded to produce the six small pages upon which the contents were printed. Despite the care with which these documents have been treated, time has made the pages brittle and fragile; the print is fading and in places all but obscured. Nothing can restore them to their original condition. Even so, a concerted effort has made it possible to republish for the first time since 1865 Simms's full account of the capture, sack, and destruction of Columbia, as it appeared originally in the *Columbia Phoenix*. It would be difficult to overestimate the value of this collection of source materials, which provided its small group of readers with the most comprehensive account of the burning of Columbia to appear in any newspaper, North or South. Written prior to the end of the war, this report remains a prime example of the South's dedication to freedom of speech and to freedom of the press. In it Simms took to task leaders in the South as well as the North with an impartiality Northern newspaper editors no longer dared to assume unless they were prepared to spend time in jail.

Deeply divided from the start, Northern newspapers were waging wars of their own. The abolitionist press raked over the coals those newspapers not firmly behind their movement. Just as there were Southern newspapers for and against the Jefferson Davis administration, so there were Northern newspapers for and against the Lincoln administration. The Republican newspapers lashed out at the Democratic newspapers. The Democratic newspapers attacked the newspapers supporting the Lincoln administration. In the South, dissenting voices were generally tolerated, even when not appreciated. In the North, the story was different. There the first casualties of war were freedom of speech and freedom of the press.

In his *Lincoln: The Man* (1931) Kansas-born lawyer and writer Edgar Lee Masters discusses the power Lincoln usurped between the time he took the oath of office in March 1861 and the time Congress met on 4 July 1861. Masters points out that, when Congress convened, Lincoln "had an army at his back; he had public discussion, free speech and a free press strangled, and he was master of the lives of men under the laws of piracy for trying to run the blockade."[1]

Simms knew about war protesters in the North, although he may not have known how many there were or how early they were escorted to prisons. According to Masters,

> By the end of September, Fort Lafayette was crowded with prisoners made such by Lincoln's mere word. Another prison had to be prepared for the hundreds gathered in for uttering so-called disloyal sentiments, for criticizing Lincoln, for displaying a Confederate flag, for anything that displeased an upstart military officer. And so the overplus was sent to Fort Warren in Boston Harbor. Hundreds of men seized on these pretexts were crowded into the Old Capital Prison at Washington, at Camp Chase in Ohio, Cairo in Illinois, at St. Louis and at Alton. In some of these prisons men were packed

almost to suffocation, some in irons and without beds, and without sufficient ventilation. Thus the republic of Washington and Jefferson vanished.[2]

How could Simms hope to escape a similar fate should Union troops return to establish official military control over Columbia? He had to make haste in putting his account before the public while it was still possible. Simms knew that the infamous General Benjamin Franklin "Spoons" Butler had, among other things, shackled the press completely when he took command of New Orleans in May 1862. Furthermore the threat of troops returning to Columbia had been made real by none other than General Oliver O. Howard when replying to a citizen's complaint of Columbia's treatment: "It is her fit punishment, and if this does not quiet rebellion, and we have to return, we will do this work thoroughly. We will not leave woman or child."[3] The warning, coming as it did from the commander of the Army of Tennessee, who was known to be a devout churchgoer opposed to drinking and gambling among his men, was as shocking as it was threatening.

The Reverend James L. Vallandigham, brother of Congressman Clement L. Vallandigham of Ohio, wrote in *The Life of Clement L. Vallandigham* (1872) that the congressman opposed the Lincoln administration and strongly defended freedom of speech and freedom of the press. As a result, he was arrested, tried, convicted, and banished from the Union with Lincoln's approval, all in 1863. According to James Vallandigham, "When the war commenced, a reign of terror was inaugurated all over the land. Freedom of speech and of the press was for awhile entirely suppressed." He reported that for a period in 1862 moderation prevailed but only briefly. By 1863 suppression returned and remained in full force through the war and thereafter: "Arbitrary arrests took place all over the country. Democratic speakers were mobbed, Democratic meetings were suppressed, and hundreds of Democrats all over the country were imprisoned, and some murdered in cold blood, for no other reason than because they were Democrats and refused to assent to the policy of the then existing Administration."[4]

Simms, like newspaper editors throughout the South, was familiar with Vallandigham's story, for it was to the South that Lincoln had banished Vallandigham. The Ohio congressman did not remain in the South; he managed to run the blockade and wound up in Canada, where he established headquarters opposite Detroit and campaigned for the governorship of Ohio, receiving in 1863 "a larger vote by many thousands than had ever been given to a Democratic candidate for Governor of Ohio."[5] The more than thirty thousand votes he received were cast in vain. Safely out of Lincoln's reach in Canada, he remained a thorn in the president's side, no doubt feeling freer to speak his mind in Canada. He risked re-arrest when of his own accord he returned to Ohio in 1864.

If Simms suspected the South was about to lose the war, he did not share that suspicion with his readers when he began writing his account of the burning of Columbia for the *Phoenix*. He took full advantage of the rights he retained as a man still free of Union control. With no one to suppress his freedom of speech or the freedom of the press in Columbia, he wrote with such power that his first biographer later declared, "Simms never wrote anything more graphic than this account of what he had seen and heard." The same biographer insisted, "It is hard to read his stirring pages without coming to the conclusion that the sack of Columbia is one of the greatest crimes ever perpetrated by the troops of a civilized country."[6]

Simms's account of the destruction of Columbia is as remarkable for what it leaves out as for what it includes. He did not, for instance, describe the advanced culture and natural beauty of Columbia prior to the invasion. He supplied no history of its progress from frontier town to handsome capital. Not once did Simms mention how familiar he was with the city, which he had frequently visited throughout his adult life. Nor did he list his qualifications to render this account in order that "our sons may always remember, and the whole Christian world everywhere may read."[7]

Each omission can be understood. Simms was writing a newspaper account for readers who knew him, knew his poetry, fiction, and nonfiction, and were already familiar with the state's history. He felt no need to waste precious space on anything other than the essentials of the immediate story. Had the South won independence, there would be no need to fill in the blanks Simms left. The history, culture, and beauty of Columbia would without a doubt have been celebrated by Southern authors. William Gilmore Simms would have retained his reputation as one of the most talented American writers. The autobiography for which he had begun collecting materials would surely have included the many strong and lasting connections he had to the capital of his native state.

Because the South failed to win her war for independence, she became an object of scorn and ridicule. Her most talented citizens were thrust into a seemingly endless struggle simply to keep food on the table. There was little leisure to produce fine works of art. Her fascinating history and her embodiment and defense of significant American ideas were rendered all but invisible. All America came to lose more than has ever been calculated.

II.

The Capital City of South Carolina

By 1860 Columbia, South Carolina, had grown from a small frontier town to a midsized community of some eight thousand people accustomed to working together to improve their city. Large sidewalks ran beside broad streets lined with oaks and Pride of India trees, commonly known as chinaberries. Magnolias and palmettos, as well as date palms and fig trees, could be found in private gardens, where clipped evergreen hedges, elaborate flower beds, and elegant water fountains contributed greatly to the capital's natural beauty.

Signs of high culture were everywhere apparent. Gas lighting was commonplace. The waterworks built in 1820 provided an abundant and dependable supply of safe water, although many residents continued to use their own wells. Three railroad lines connected the city to Charleston, Greenville, and Charlotte. The telegraph linked Columbia to the rest of the country and made the swift transmission of news possible, greatly benefiting the several newspapers published in the capital.

In *Columbia: Portrait of a City* (1986) Walter B. Edgar and Deborah K. Woolley maintain that in 1860 "almost any service or product could be found that a Columbian or visitor might desire." The city had four major hotels, eleven boardinghouses, ten churches, three carriage manufacturers, two planing mills, two iron factories, two breweries, and thirteen lawyers. According to Edgar and Woolley, "Small shops lined both sides of Richardson Street: from bakers, booksellers, and clothiers to florists, grocers, and upholsterers."[8]

The first State House, which was destroyed by Sherman's troops, was one of the most interesting buildings then in Columbia. In *Architecture of the Old South: South Carolina* (1984) Mills Lane declared, "It has been conjectured that the first State House at Columbia may have been designed by the Irish-born architect James Hoban (c. 1756–1821), who had come to Philadelphia soon after the Revolution and reached Charleston (the name of the city was changed from Charles Town in 1783) by May, 1790, when he opened an evening school, for the instruction of young men in architecture." Lane went on to say, "Like Hoban's famous 1793 design for the President's House at Washington, the Columbia State House could have been easily mistaken for a mid-18th century English Palladian country house." Lane's description of the building as "a frame structure on a low brick foundation with a pedimented portico and a wood shingle roof painted brown" is augmented by a comment in the diary of Edward Hooker, who asserted in 1805 that several rooms of the lower story were used for little else than lodging goats that ran loose on the streets and could enter the building at will because its doors were never shut.[9] Despite these uncomplimentary descriptions, the State House appears impressive in drawings made of it during the 1800s. As for the presence of goats roaming the streets of Columbia in 1805, it is worth remembering that New York newspapers were reporting problems presented by pigs running wild on the streets of New York as late as the 1870s.

Attributing its design to Hoban, Edgar and Woolley have presented a more positive picture of the first State House, declaring that its construction predated the building of the White House and asserting: "The White House in Washing-ton, D.C., is a carbon copy of South Carolina's first State House in Columbia." They also reported, "This would not be the last time that an architectural idea was used first in South Carolina's new capital and later used in the nation's capi-tal."[10] In *Sherman and the Burning of Columbia* (1976) Marion Brunson Lucas wrote of Columbia's growth and noted, "In 1854 the deteriorating sixty-four-year-old wooden building that had served as the state house for South Carolina was moved to the northeast corner of Assembly and Senate streets to make room for a magnificent new granite structure at the head of Richardson Street."[11] That it was moved rather than destroyed indicates the building was deemed either worthy of saving or still of use to the city. It must have been a sturdy structure, for it not only survived the move but also was still in use in 1865, twelve years later.

Another description of the State House comes from F. Y. Hedley, who in 1884 remembered it as "dingy and forbidding." His position as adjutant of the 32nd Illinois Infantry probably colored his description. Hedley was with the first Union detachment to plant its flags upon the old State House. The new state capitol still was under construction. In *Marching through Georgia* (written in 1884, published in 1890) Hedley devoted a chapter to the capture of Columbia, beginning with what he saw from the west bank of the Congaree River:

> On the opposite side, on ground gently sloping to the river, lay Columbia, its wide streets, wealth of ornamental trees, and handsome buildings, mak-ing a picture charming to the eye. The imposing walls of the new capitol, yet unfinished, rose in massive beauty; the white marble of column and cornice —each stone was said to have cost a round thousand dollars—glittering in the sunlight like immense gems. Near this magnificent edifice stood its less conspicuous neighbor, the old capitol, dingy and forbidding.[12]

The old capitol did not seem dingy and forbidding to Emma LeConte, who wrote of it in her wartime diary, later published as *When the World Ended* (1957). She wrote at length of the last big community event that took place within its walls before it was destroyed. The Ladies' Bazaar, a grand affair held to raise funds for sick and wounded soldiers of the Confederacy, opened on 18 January 1865: "The tables or booths are tastefully draped with damask and lace curtains, and elaborately decorated with evergreens. To go in there one would scarce believe it was war times."[13] After Sherman's troops left the city, Emma went out to see what was left of it and lamented, "As we passed the old State House going back, I paused to gaze on the ruins—only the foundations and chimneys—and to recall the brilliant scene enacted there one short month ago. And I com-pared that scene with its beauty, gaiety and festivity—the halls so elaborately decorated, the surging throng—with this. I reached home sad at heart and full of all I had seen."[14]

The first State House had been built after the War for American Independence. It had been visited by George Washington, who was entertained there in 1791 at a dinner held in his honor. It was only one of many buildings signifying Columbia's advanced and developing culture; many were destroyed; some survived.

In 1836 Robert Mills of South Carolina was appointed Architect of Public Buildings by President Andrew Jackson. Under Hoban's influence, Mills became the designer of the Washington Monument, as well as the Washington, D.C., Post Office, Patent Office, and Treasury Building. In 1800 Mills had followed Hoban to Washington, when Hoban was in charge of building the U.S. Capitol. What the nineteen-year-old South Carolina–born architect and future pupil of Thomas Jefferson learned from Hoban can be seen in the design for South Carolina College in Columbia, a plan Mills submitted in 1802. While elements of Mills's design, "were incorporated into the final scheme, and it appears that Mills was then hired to make final drawings for the College buildings,"[15] his more complete and lasting influence on Columbia's architecture was not made until after he had spent considerable time in acquainting himself with Thomas Jefferson's architectural tastes. According to Lane, "Jefferson encouraged the young Carolinian's ambitions by hiring him to make drawings for additions to Monticello, Jefferson's home near Charlottesville, Virginia, and allowing Mills to use his architecture library, probably the finest collection in the country at the time."[16] Mills and Jefferson exchanged letters until Jefferson's death in 1826.

Robert Mills's connection with South Carolina College is significant. It establishes Columbia's early interest in and support of a youthful and native talent. It also closely links the concerns of the state to a concern for the proposed college the state had committed itself to support. Mills was able to use his obviously advanced skills as a draftsman to make the final drawings of the buildings. Thus the trustees were able to progress rapidly from design to construction, making possible the January 1805 opening of South Carolina College, just three years after its establishment by the state legislature on December 19, 1801, in compliance with the wishes of the citizens who were committed to higher education. More important, Mills's initial interest in the college was part of his even greater interest in Columbia's civic projects in general, the end result being his intimate involvement in the capital's architectural heritage.

By 1854 South Carolina College had a faculty equal to that of any college in the South or in the country as a whole. It was the first American college endowed completely by a state from its own resources, and, according to Daniel Walker Hollis it had the "first separate college library building in the United

States." By 1850 that library held 18,400 volumes, more than were held in the libraries of Princeton or Columbia. Even though "the official records do not substantiate"[17] that Robert Mills was the architect of the college library or was even consulted about the building plans, "a surviving diary of Mills indicates that he was involved in its planning."[18] A 27 January 1837 sketch by Mills for the college library is in the Library of Congress, and as Lane has reported, "Another Mills drawing, a more polished version of one of his plans, has been found at the Library itself."[19] Certainly the finished library building displays many of the elements incorporated in Mills's drawings for the college library.

Additional research and careful reading of books and diaries written by Mills reveal that he lived on "the southeast corner of Pendleton and Sumter streets, facing the university"[20] from 1821 to 1825. Mills was a member and elder of the First Presbyterian Church when John Smith Mills, his only male relative, was buried in 1822 in the church cemetery. This child was less than two years old and except for his grave stone, there are no Mills markers to be found in the cemetery. A comprehensive list of campus-related materials can be found in Mills's writings. He had "ample opportunity to inspect the buildings and grounds." Brick structures included two ranges, three stories high for student dormitories, studies, lecture room, and chapel as well as a president's house, four houses for professors, and a large building with a laboratory, a library, and lecture and mineralogical rooms within its walls. A steward's house, refectory, and an octagon observatory completed the outer square, which contained the ten acres known as the campus. Since the library was not yet located in a separate building, Mills was describing the campus as it existed prior to 1840.[21]

Mills likely designed the DeBruhl-Marshall House in Columbia on Laurel at Marion Street, which was used as headquarters in 1865 by Union General James A. Johnstone. The two and a half acre L-shaped grounds at the rear of the house were once fruit and vegetable gardens. English boxwood shrubs planted alongside the brick walls when the house was new endured long after the fruit and vegetable gardens were gone.[22]

Mills designed the Ainsley Hall House for his friend and fellow church member Ainsley Hall, who died before it was completed in 1825 without incorporation of the original plans of its interior. Located on Blanding Street, it was sold to the Presbyterian Church in 1829 and was home to the Columbia Theological Seminary from 1830 to 1927. Another Mills contribution to Columbia's architecture was St. Peter's Catholic Church on Assembly Street, which was dedicated in 1830 and enlarged in 1858. Mills Lane's book contains a photograph of the impressive structure, which was demolished in 1908.[23]

Many scholars have paid tribute to one of Robert Mills's most remarkable Columbia buildings. Sometimes called the State Hospital and sometimes the

State Asylum, the Lunatic Asylum of Columbia was attracting the favorable attention of visitors long before 1860. Nothing quite like it had ever been built in America to serve the needs of mentally distressed people. Dedicated as he was to the humane treatment of the mentally ill, Mills combined elegance, permanence, economy, and security in its design. Iron bars were made to look like window sashes. Secret hinges and locks erased the temptation to make an escape. Fireproofing measures in the building's construction were supplemented by a central fire escape, which served as a stairway to the upper floors. Beautiful inside and out, the building had a copper-covered roof and the country's first roof garden. Rooms for patients opened on the "sunny southside"[24] of the building and looked down on an ornamental garden. Completed in 1827, the asylum became the sixth such building in the country and the only one made fireproof at the time. Spacious corridors, hospitals, refectories, a medical hall, several parlors, keepers' apartments, kitchens, accommodations for 120 patients and sundry offices were incorporated into Mills's original structure, which was added to in later years.

Columbia may have been architecturally elegant even if Robert Mills had never contributed anything to its supply of remarkable buildings. He was, after all, working on projects that had to meet with the approval of Columbians who reviewed his proposals. Still, it can't be denied that his name and growing reputation made what he designed more valuable in the eyes of people far removed from South Carolina's capital. That he was appreciated and supported by his own people says as much about them as it does about Robert Mills.

The cultural community in Columbia did not restrict itself to supporting architects. It included serious art collectors as well. The artist James DeVeaux received financial support from Columbia patrons such as Robert Gibbes, Wade Hampton II, and John Preston, who also assisted Hiram Powers, the nationally acclaimed antebellum sculptor. DeVeaux is best known for his portraits of upcountry Carolinians. Preserving an image of an esteemed family member and passing that image down from generation to generation helped to ensure family continuity and to provide a source for family veneration. Perhaps love of family is the reason Louisa Cheves McCord, one of the most intellectual women writers in the antebellum South, had her portrait painted in Columbia in 1853 by her neighbor William Harrison Scarborough, and later sat for Hiram Powers while she was in Florence, Italy, in 1859. Love of family is certainly the reason she commissioned Powers to produce a bust of her father, Langdon Cheves, who had been speaker of the House of Representatives before President James Monroe appointed him president in 1819 of the Bank of the United States. Financial support provided by Columbia's art patrons had made it possible for both DeVeaux and Powers to study abroad.

Although America was itself a young republic in 1860, the city of Columbia was even younger. It was peopled with talented individuals, who in the wake of winning their independence from the British Empire were building a civilization and establishing regional resources in order to free themselves of dependency on others. Mirroring the energy and enthusiasm of Charlestonians, as described by artist Charles Fraser in his *Reminiscences of Charleston* (1854),[25] upcountry Carolinians were producing painters to depict surrounding landscapes and writers to create a distinctively Southern American literature. Columbia educators were providing schools in which to train future leaders, thereby releasing parents from the stresses and burdens of sending sons to Europe or to the North.

Established exactly ten years after the British had evacuated Charleston, the Columbia Male Academy had been in existence since 1792. The Arsenal Academy was established in 1842, the same year the Citadel was created in Charleston. Both provided young men the military training needed to defend the state. Academies for young women and home schooling became common. The South Carolina Female Collegiate Institute had opened in Columbia in 1829. The Columbia Female Academy had been established almost fifteen years earlier. Writing in his *Reminiscences* of growing up and living in Charleston, Charles Fraser remembered as many as fourteen female academies in the port city. Excellent tutors could be found in many private residences. In Columbia, Louisa Cheves McCord sent her daughters three afternoons a week to the home of a Frenchwoman with whom they could practice conversing in French. She also read to them daily in French and English and ordered children's books in both French and German, books they could read on their own.

Puritan values had never taken hold in South Carolina. Consequently Columbia, like Charleston, had a variety of Christian churches and a sprinkling of Jewish congregations, all with strong ties to their communities. "By midcentury Baptist, Episcopalians, Lutherans, Methodists, Presbyterians, and Roman Catholics had built substantial houses of worship. There was also a Hebrew Benevolent Society."[26] The Ursuline Convent and Academy had accommodations for two hundred pupils. St. Mary's College, another Catholic institution, had accommodations for one hundred students. Methodists had sponsored the Columbia Female College, and the Presbyterian Church had established the Columbia Theological Seminary.

Distinguished scientists working in Columbia made their own contributions to the city. Joseph LeConte and his brother John taught at South Carolina College. Joseph was a professor of chemistry with a love for literature and art. He tutored his daughter Emma in Latin, Greek, French, German, and mathematics. John was a professor of natural and mechanical philosophy. His lovely wife, Josephine, entertained members of the legislature, who gathered around her tea table and greatly admired her charm. The brothers were later given commissions as majors in the Confederacy and "rendered valuable service in developing sources of scarce minerals such as lead and saltpeter."[27]

Another distinguished scientist, Robert W. Gibbes, gave even more to the community. He taught chemistry, geology, and mineralogy at South Carolina College. He received a degree from the Medical College of South Carolina in Charleston but continued to teach at South Carolina College until he started his medical practice in Columbia at the age of twenty-three. He wrote monographs in his field and compiled the *Documentary History of the American Revolution* (1853). As a collector he had no equal in Columbia. He gathered fossils, minerals, scientific documents, and historical documents with the same passion he displayed in collecting more than two hundred works of art by leading painters and sculptors. He became mayor of Columbia and a proprietor of the *South Carolinian.* Richard B. McCaslin included a photograph of Gibbes in his *Portrait of Conflict: A Photographic History of South Carolina in the Civil War* (1994) and noted, "In the summer of 1861 he accepted an appointment as an inspector of hospitals for the Confederate army." He served as "surgeon general of South Carolina until the end of the war."[28]

Gibbes was the father of seven sons. His youngest, Benjamin, became a lieutenant in the 16th South Carolina Infantry and was posted in Georgia; as McCaslin notes, "He did not receive a single paycheck before dying of typhoid fever at home in Columbia."[29] He was not yet eighteen when he died on 14 March 1864.

Another son, Wade Hampton Gibbes, attended the Citadel, graduated from West Point in 1860, and became a major in the Confederacy, serving in South Carolina, North Carolina, and Virginia. Multitalented like his father, Wade Gibbes became a farmer, a railroad contractor, a treasurer of Richland County, a postmaster at Columbia, a bank vice president, and finally the president of a wine company before his death at age sixty-six.

Although much has been written about stored alcohol in Columbia near the end of the war, little has surfaced about the budding wine industry in the state. James Everett Kibler discovered that Simms planted two thousand grape vines at Woodlands on the advice of James Henry Hammond. Hammond and the noted horticulturist-scientist Henry William Ravenel were ardent vine culturists, whose "object was to encourage a good local wine industry using the native grapes like the Warren and Catawba."[30] South Carolina's support of a wine industry survived the war, as seen in McCaslin's mention of Wade Gibbes as the president of a wine company and in McCaslin's mention of South Carolinian John J. Lucas, who after the war "became noted as a wine maker and served as president of the Darlington Agricultural and Mechanical Fair Company."[31]

While New England Puritans may have objected to Columbia's appreciation of spirited beverages, the interest had a long history and a European connection. In *Dutch Fork Cookery* (1989) Juanita Kibler included recipes used in the German kitchens of South Carolinians as far back as the eighteenth century. Special occasion beverages such as persimmon beer, rice wine, blackberry wine, scuppernong wine, muscadine wine, and hot buttered rum mull—the "favorite Christmas drink of the earliest days"[32]—were all made at home and clearly associated with either social or sacred celebrations. Two of her recipes were used for the production of communion wine in Lutheran churches. Others—like that for sangaree, which was "the favorite drink at wedding celebrations in the early 1800s and earlier," and blackberry cordial, which "was used before the War Between the States in central South Carolina"[33]—have social associations. By 1860, Columbia also had two local breweries. There is, therefore, little reason to doubt South Carolinians were testing the market for local and imported vintage wine, much of which was · stored for safety in cellars throughout the city.

Antebellum Columbia was a city of gardens and gardeners. When Alice G. B. Lockwood, chair of the special publication committee of the Garden Club of America, compiled and edited *Gardens of Colonies and of the Republic before 1840* (1934), she included two Columbia gardens visited in 1825 by His Highness, Bernard, Duke of Saxe-Weimar-Eisenach. She wrote that "Russel's Garden in Columbia was famous about a hundred years ago and was a great institution in the capital city." It was "elaborately laid out" and also had "a green house from which potted plants were sold." Children enjoyed a "handsome fountain in a very large basin." This fashionable gathering place was sacrificed to make space for the new State House. The duke was also impressed by Lyon's Garden, which once occupied a whole square. It was "laid out in long alleys" and had "a labyrinth in which the children delighted to lose themselves."[34]

Sidney Park, now called Finlay Park, was established in the early 1800s and described in the *South Carolinian* on 22 April 1864: "One of the loveliest walks or rides in Columbia is in Sidney Park and its vicinity, about the hour of 5 P.M. Nature is donning herself in her spring attire, the birds make music, the children prattle with their nurses, the young ladies enjoy flirtations with their gallants . . . in the flower-embroidered basin."[35]

The Hampton-Preston Mansion on Blanding Street and the home of David and Louisa McCord on the corner of Pendleton and Bull streets had magnificent private gardens. The McCord garden had its own greenhouse and many fountains near the main house to keep it cool in the summer. The four-acre garden of the Hampton-Preston Mansion was planted with magnolias, boxwood, camellias, tea olives, deodar cedars, azaleas, and rare exotic tropicals. Henry

Wright, a soldier of the 6th Iowa who was an eyewitness to the burning of Columbia, lamented the loss of so much beauty: "All officers and men who had a keen sense of appreciation for the charming loveliness and tropical splendor of the yards and grounds, forests of ornamental trees interwoven with bowers of twining vines and flowering shrubbery and beautiful gardens were filled with a genuine sense of sadness and deep-felt regret at the wanton destruction of such rare and beautiful property."[36] Nearby Millwood Plantation, home of General Wade Hampton III, also had splendid gardens. The thirteen-thousand-acre property included stables, where Hampton kept some of the finest horses in the country, and a racetrack enjoyed by the celebrated leader and his fellow equestrians.

The war against the South brought significant changes to Columbia as early as 1861. South Carolina College began to experience a drop in student enrollment as young men traded textbooks for guns and uniforms. On 17 March 1862 the college had only nine students; five were freshmen, and four were sophomores. By June several buildings on campus were diverted to use by the Confederacy and were turned over to the Confederate medical director. The hospital set up by a medical unit needed more and more space as the number of wounded Southerners increased. Because the campus buildings were used as a hospital where both Confederate and Union soldiers were convalescing, when Sherman invaded Columbia, the college was saved from destruction by fire.

The city of Columbia grew in population even though its young men were leaving and dying in record numbers. Wives and widows of Confederate soldiers were employed to produce currency and bonds when the Confederate printing operations were moved in 1862 from Richmond to Columbia. The largest medical manufacturing facility in the Confederacy was set up by Joseph LeConte at the city's old fairgrounds. To keep pace with the demand for woolen cloth, the Saluda Factory employed one thousand workers. Factories producing socks, shoes, uniforms, hats, and even buttons for the army were soon in operation. Cannons, cannonballs, swords, and bayonets were being produced in Columbia's foundries. Each of these war-related enterprises brought to the capital additional residents until its prewar population of eight thousand had grown to a population of almost twenty-five thousand.

Wounded soldiers, as well as boys too young and men too old or too ill for military service, made up the largest portion of the city's male population. The number of widows in the female population increased, as did the number of wives with husbands on distant battlefields. Because Columbia was considered a safe haven, refugees poured into the capital even as Sherman's troops drew closer. By 1864 financial distress was widespread; the Board of Relief found itself with more than eleven hundred people in need of assistance. Southerners were losing their property and their homes. Those with resources shared, and charity never faltered.

Southern women later told their experiences of the horrors of invasion, many in the *South Carolina News and Courier.* One account by a woman identified only by her initials, A.P.S., begins with the writer's circumstances on 17 February 1865: "After the evacuation of Columbia by the Confederates, my father being absent in the Government service, we like many others were left without a protector and at the mercy of the enemy, then pouring by the thousands into our town." She told of walking with her sick mother, three siblings, and "fifty women and children" to the northern part of town after her own home was set on fire. Her first night of homelessness was spent in an open square. The next two days and nights were spent at the Lunatic Asylum, where homeless wanderers were being sheltered and fed by Dr. Parker, the superintendent. The family was found by two of their servants, one of whom offered them a house "given to him by the Yankees." Plundered and left with only a bench and a bedstead, the house nevertheless provided shelter. There the family was found by "Mr. J. J. McCarter, loaded with biscuits his wife had made and sent to us." Next came Mr. Alfred Huger, who found some "rusty dishcovers" they could use for holding well water to wash their faces. He also volunteered shards of "his once elegant mirror," which had been converted to any number of looking glasses by "Yankee ingenuity." Mayor Thomas J. Goodwyn later "took out his handkerchief with his share of meal . . . one pint . . . and handed it to mother." Speaking of the generosity of the women of Columbia, the writer insisted, "No one was so poor as not to be able to give from her little stock." When her mother's illness became known, a friend delivered to the family "a small flask of brandy, a little bag of flour and a cup of loaf sugar." As soon as the friend left, the writer's mother repacked these "precious things" and sent them to a "sufferer more in need of them." On a humorous note, the writer added, "Delicacies made at a sacrifice for the sick were sent from one friend to another until they reached the original source."[37]

Sherman's invasion of South Carolina left a hunger for more than food. In another newspaper account, Miss Claudine Rhett of Charleston stated, "We hungered and thirsted for information in regard to the tide of war more than for any material sustenance." She emphasized her point by adding, "I do not believe there was a woman in the Confederate States, after the hard fighting had begun, who, having to make a choice, would not any day have preferred a newspaper to her dinner."[38] Those hungry for news before Sherman's capture of Columbia were all but starved for information by the time William Gilmore Simms began editing the *Columbia Phoenix*, a month after Sherman and his troops left the city.

III.

William Gilmore Simms (17 April 1806–11 June 1870)

Prior to the Confederate War, William Gilmore Simms was one of the best known and most highly respected authors in America. He had won a name for himself for his fiction, nonfiction, and poetry in both the North and the South. No writer in this country was more prolific. None could claim a body of published works more diverse. By the beginning of the war Simms had already produced twenty-eight novels, four short-story collections, nineteen volumes of poetry, two of drama, five biographies, three histories, five volumes of miscellanies, four of reviews, five orations published in book form, and a geography of South Carolina.

Impressive as these numbers are, they do not include the time and effort Simms had spent on editorial duties. In 1825–26 he wrote for and coedited the *Album*, perhaps the South's first literary magazine. In 1828 he cofounded, wrote for, and helped to edit the *Southern Literary Gazette*, becoming its sole editor in 1829. He edited the *Charleston City Gazette*, a daily newspaper, from 1830 to 1832. In 1833 he wrote for and coedited the *Cosmopolitan: An Occasional*. He subsequently edited the *Magnolia; or Southern Appalachian* (1842–1843), *Orion; or, Southern Monthly* (1844), the *Southern and Western Monthly Magazine and Review* (1845), and the *Southern Quarterly Review* (1849–1855). From 1854 to 1856 and again from 1858 to 1860 he was book-review editor for the *Charleston Mercury*. He also gave his support to friend and fellow poet Paul Hamilton Hayne during Hayne's editorship of *Russell's Magazine*, which was published in Charleston from 1857 to 1860.

Reviewed, acclaimed, and quoted, Simms had written works that by 1860 were found in the country's major anthologies, short-story collections, gift books, and annuals. Books by Simms were translated into German. He had a British following and as early as the 1830s was favorably reviewed by Thomas Campbell in the *London Metropolitan Magazine*. One of his most enduring short-story collections, *The Wigwam and the Cabin . . . First Series* (1845), was published in 1848 in Aberdeen, Scotland, as *Life in America*.

Generally speaking, Simms knew where his volumes were sold throughout this and other countries. It is unlikely, though, that he knew some of his works had reached Russia. No mention of a Russian readership can be found in the six-volume collection of his letters. Yet, according to the Russian scholars Professor E. A. Morozkina and postgraduate student M. O. Erchtein, "The leading Russian libraries in Moscow and St. Petersburg bought Simms's novels published from the 1850s through the 1880s." The books, which are part of rare-book collections, are now on display in both libraries. Morozkina and Erchtein, who belong to the "Russian circle of Simms's devotees" formed in the 1980s, note, "In 1850 the magazine *Pantheon and Repertoire of the Russian Stage* first mentioned Simms as 'the most prolific American writer along with J. F. Cooper, amazing and remarkable.'" Considered a prominent Southern American writer by Russian critics and readers, Simms was also mentioned in the 1855 edition of *Library for Reading* and the 1882 edition of *The History of World Literature*, collected by V. Zotor and published in Moscow and St. Petersburg.[39]

Simms was an author of remarkable genius capable of producing books that appealed to a wide variety of readers. In this country alone his volumes were published in Charleston, New York, Boston, Philadelphia, Richmond, and Baltimore. His ever expanding circle of friends included politicians, preachers, painters, physicians, musicians, actors, scientists, merchants, bankers, and college professors. The number of personal letters he wrote staggers the imagination, especially since most were handwritten late at night by candlelight when his wife and children were fast asleep.

Although Simms was widely read by the men of his day, he appealed to a female readership as well. He was a faithful contributor to the *Southern Rose*, a woman's periodical published by his friend Caroline Gilman. He also contributed to *Godey's*, a woman's periodical published by Louis Antonine Godey and edited by Mrs. Sarah Josepha Hale. Because Godey and Mrs. Hale gave American women what they most wanted to read, the 1851 circulation of *Godey's* was twice that of any other American periodical.

Simms, who was sketched, painted, and photographed by some of America's leading artists, stood almost six feet tall in his prime. Blue eyed, clean-shaven, and well muscled, he adopted a conservative, yet fashionable, clothing style as suitable in the North as it was in the South. Unlike the sometimes rumpled Edgar Allan Poe and the always flamboyantly dressed Charles Dickens, Simms managed to blend in successfully whenever he appeared in public.

One of the best portraits of Simms was done in 1844 by William Edward West, who had studied with the celebrated artist Thomas Sully. West became famous in Europe for his portraits of Byron, Shelley, and Trelawney. A handsome caricature of Simms done by Charles Martin appeared in the 5 December 1846 issue of *Yankee Doodle*. The caricature and a paragraph quoted from Simm's *Guy Rivers* (1834) were used to introduce a short commentary that included the following: "It is certainly true—and *Yankee Doodle* records the fact to the disgrace of the North—that literary men and editors at the South seldom indulge in the scurrility, envious malignity and persevering misrepresentations which, too often here, form the weapons with which men who write, propel their crazy vehicles along the crowded and dusty avenues to fame and distinction."[40]

Another likeness of Simms was sketched by Henry Brintwell Bounethease in 1853. An engraved portrait based on this sketch appeared in a volume of poetry published in the same year. The unknown engraver who produced his own likeness of Simms for volume 3 of the *Cosmopolitan Art Journal* (1859) was guided, at the author's request, by a photograph supplied by Simms and an engraved portrait previously published by Simms's New York publisher, Redfield. The modern celebrity who requests an air brushing of his photograph to obtain a more polished appearance in the media would no doubt understand the instructions Simms gave to the art journal's editor, Orville James Victor: "Your engraver will need to open the eyes a little."[41]

Exactly where Simms learned to conduct a successful public-relations campaign is not known. He may have acquired the knowledge piecemeal from friends in his literary circle, which included fellow novelist James Fenimore Cooper and fellow poets William Cullen Bryant and Fitz-Greene Halleck. Two of his closest friends in New York, James Lawson and Evert Augustus Duyckinck, were certainly invaluable guides since both were well versed in the city's publishing practices. Duyckinck not only included Simms in the *Cyclopedia of American Literature* (1854) but also sought his advice for much of the Southern material it contained. Lawson, on the other hand, became more of a personal rather than professional friend and honored the relationship by doing those chores commonly performed today by literary agents. Simms may have learned a good deal by simply observing the literary progress of friends such as Edgar Allan Poe and Washington Irving.

In observing Irving, Simms probably learned the importance of conciliations and successful networking. The still popular and often reproduced painting *Washington Irving and His Literary Friends at Sunnyside* (1863) shows Simms seated in the foreground and to the far left of Irving. The artist, Christian Schussele, placed his subjects in a casual atmosphere of comfort and compatibility. The fifteen American authors included are Henry T. Tuckerman, Oliver Wendell Holmes, Simms, Fitz-Greene Halleck, Nathaniel Hawthorne, Henry Wadsworth Longfellow, Nathaniel Parker Willis, William H. Prescott, Washington Irving, James K. Paulding, Ralph Waldo Emerson, William Cullen Bryant, John P. Kennedy, James Fenimore Cooper, and George Bancroft. An engraving of Schussele's painting was promised to Simms by James Cephas Derby.

In 1866 Simms asked Duyckinck to procure the engraving from Derby, publisher of the *Cosmopolitan Art Journal*. The following year, in a letter to John Jacob Bockee, Simms said of the engraving, "The picture of Irving, etc. will help to cover the bomb-shell holes in our walls."[42] The New Yorkers Bockee and Duyckinck aided Simms in procuring shelter for his family after the war by facilitating the sale of Simms's collection of Revolutionary War documents to the Long Island Historical Society.

In observing his less successful friend Poe, Simms probably learned how easily a public-relations campaign could be tarnished by inappropriate personal conduct. He often found himself in the awkward position of defending Poe to the very Northern associates he had once asked to befriend the talented but mercurial author. When Poe wrote asking for advice on his troubled affairs, Simms was forced to admonish him to stop squabbling and to rid himself of undesirable associates.

Readers familiar with the face of Simms were equally familiar with his penmanship. Facsimiles of his signature frequently accompanied his published portraits, and engraved reproductions of a manuscript page occasionally appeared as well. An early example of the tactfulness Simms employed in dealing with what can only be described as fan mail also serves to demonstrate his working knowledge of the long-term value of an author's autograph.

In 1837 a gentleman named Joseph B. Boyd wrote to Simms from Cincinnati with a request for verses. Simms began his response with an apology for his three-month delay in answering. He then went on to say, "However, willing, and pleased, to serve those who think kindly of my labors in the literary world, I should be reluctant, on a sudden, to write verses for one who thinks so highly of my capacities. I am quite satisfied to have secured your favorable opinion, and you must excuse me, my dear Sir, if I decline risking what I have already secured, by an undue or precipitate effort, even if taken to oblige. I can not send you the verses you desire, but the autograph is at your service."[43] If Boyd was disappointed by his failure to obtain verses written by Simms, he was nevertheless in possession of a celebrated American author's autograph as well as a letter of appreciation personally addressed to him.

As an avid collector of autographs and manuscripts of Revolutionary War figures, Simms knew the potential value of something as seemingly insignificant as a simple original signature. His dedication to historical accuracy when writing either poetry or prose had led to an early desire for ready access to primary source materials. Letters, journals, and other documents related to the War for American Independence were of special interest to him when he began his collection of manuscripts in the mid 1830s. Membership in historical societies, correspondence with fellow historians, and a great deal of independent research enabled him to acquire a personal archive of which he was justifiably proud.

George Washington, Patrick Henry, John Adams, John Jay, Thomas Paine, Francis Marion, John Rutledge, Baron de Kalb, Christopher Gadsden, William Moultrie, Henry Laurens, and Colonel John Laurens are some of the significant historical figures known to have been represented in Simms's collection of manuscripts. While he also added rare books and pamphlets to his library, he did not feel these additions could be favorably compared to the original manuscripts in his collection. He stressed the importance of gathering manuscripts in a letter he wrote to John Pendleton Kennedy shortly after his friend became president of the Maryland Historical Society in 1851. After expressing his belief that accumulating manuscripts should be the chief concern of historical societies, Simms declared, "Pamphlets & books are of far less importance to such a Society than private letters which, I am persuaded, are still to be dragged out of old chests & old wives closets. I have now a very valuable & numerous collection, thus obtained, the existence of which was totally unsuspected in the community."[44]

Throughout his life Simms generously shared the wealth of information he had on hand with historians who appealed to him for help with their projects. Simms also edited and published many of the documents in his possession in order that interested readers could expand their awareness of American history, especially that portion of history played out in the South during the Revolution.

The fine art of Southern hospitality was something of a specialty with Simms, whose plantation home in the Barnwell District of South Carolina was always open to visitors. Following his move to Georgia in 1838, the London-born artist T. A. Richards was several times a Simms guest. Richards made his first visit to Simms's plantation, Woodlands, in 1844, when he was twenty-four years old. In 1852 Richards made a graphite sketch that S. V. Hunt then used as a model for the steel engraving of Woodlands, which appeared in *Homes of American Authors* before year's end. In 1857 Richards's account of a visit to Woodlands was published in *Appletons' Illustrated Hand-Book of American Travels: A Full and Reliable Guide to Railway, Steamboat, and Stage.*

A much earlier visitor, William Cullen Bryant, wrote a letter from Barnwell in 1843, describing his visit to Simms. It was published in Bryant's *Letters of a Traveller* (1850). A shorter version of the account was published in volume 3 of Evert Duyckinck's *Cyclopedia of American Literature* in 1856.

John Pendleton Kennedy was another friend and writer warmly received at Woodlands. Born in Baltimore and best known as the author of *Swallow Barn* (1832) and *Horse-Shoe Robinson* (1835), Kennedy was also a lawyer and politician who served several terms as a member of the Maryland House of Delegates. After serving as speaker of the House of Delegates, he became a member of Congress and was later named secretary of the navy.

Simms was frequently compared to the prolific British author George Payne Rainsford James. Like Simms, James wrote historical romances that were praised both in England and in America. James briefly served as historiographer royal during the reign of William IV. As British consul to America, he served in

Massachusetts and Virginia. On his visit to Woodlands he was accompanied by his wife and children. The two authors corresponded for years.

Simms corresponded with the Scotsman James Lawson for forty years. Born in Glasgow, Lawson had been living in New York for seventeen years and was still a bachelor when he first met the recently widowed Simms in 1832. Lawson was a poet, playwright, newspaper editor, and businessman. Although he was seven years older than Simms, the two became close friends and spent the next few summers courting some of New York's most fashionable young ladies. When Lawson became engaged to Mary Eliza Donaldson in 1835, Simms was in South Carolina contemplating a second marriage. He proposed to Chevillette Eliza Roach of Orangeburg District and was accepted. By the end of 1836, both Lawson and Simms were married men. Their wives became friends, and then their children became such devoted friends that visiting between New York and Woodlands grew commonplace until the war.

The final Lawson visits to Woodlands prior to the war were in 1860. James Lawson and his daughters Mary and Kate visited in early 1860. James Lawson Jr. came to spend time with William Gilmore Simms Jr. ten months later. Jimmy arrived on Wednesday, 5 December, and was off on a partridge hunt with Gilmore two days later. On 13 December, the boys traveled to nearby Barnwell for a five-day round of deer hunting, horseback riding, dinners, and evening parties. They were guests in the home of Alfred Proctor Aldrich, a member of the South Carolina Legislature. While there, Jimmy wrote to his sister Christina, "I have had plenty of dinner parties, two at Gen Jamison's (who will be the Governor of the Republic of So. Ca.) so you see I have been living on the fat of the land. . . . Tonight the Aldriches will have a tea party. I am very anxious to go to the Convention which meets on Monday, they will vote the State out of the Union on Tuesday, and I think it will be a very solemn and imposing ceremony."[45]

Jimmy Lawson returned to Woodlands to find more visitors had arrived. Mr. and Mrs. Joseph Denck and their thirteen-year-old son, a musical prodigy whose performances had astonished much of Europe, were there, as well as Mrs. Jamison and all her family except for the general, who had been elected president of the convention, which had been moved from Columbia to Charleston because of an outbreak of smallpox in the capital. Jimmy was treated to a Woodlands flute and violin concert as well as a trip to Charleston for the Secession Convention. The holiday season was well underway, and the already full house at Woodlands continued to receive even more visitors. Simms was adding a library wing to the house and altering the front steps. Bricks were being made; timber was being cut from his woods; three of his beeves and six hogs were being slaughtered to provide meat for festive meals; and the plantation buzzed with excitement as South Carolina prepared to free itself from Northern domination.

On 31 December 1860, Simms wrote to Lawson about the arrangements he was making to send Jimmy home safely. Fearing the South might be on the eve of conflict and afraid the steamers in Savannah might be stopped as they had been in Charleston, Simms was making contingency plans to send Jimmy home by land. Entrusted by Simms into the care of Israel Teft in Savannah, Jimmy was, however, able to return home by sea. He was the last Lawson to visit Woodlands prior to the war and became the first Lawson to visit Woodlands after the war, when he returned to "rough it" with Gilmore in what little was left of the once fine plantation house.

In *The Dispossessed Garden* (1975) Lewis Simpson boldly declared, "As nearly as the South had a center in the Republic of Letters following the age when Monticello was such a place, Simms's plantation (called Woodlands) was it. It is hardly too much to say that in a literary sense the Age of Jefferson was succeeded by the Age of William Gilmore Simms."[46] Simpson may well have been correct. Woodlands may have been "a center in the Republic of Letters." It obviously attracted a large and influential number of literary-minded visitors. For Simms, however, Woodlands was first and foremost a home for his family, a place where he could enjoy the company of a wife he loved and respected, where he could romp with his children and argue agricultural policies with his father-in-law. In so far as he could, Simms sheltered his family from the glare of the public. When asked for biographical information, Simms provided journalists with minimal details on his personal life. Comments on his ancestry were brief. Comments on members of his immediate family were all but nonexistent. Even in personal correspondence with close friends, Simms spoke more often as author rather than as the family man who did the writing. What Simms knew of his family history and what he was willing to share with the public were in his mind very different matters. Aware that he owed his readership an honest account of who he was and where he stood on important issues, he nevertheless maintained a dignified distance between his public and his private life. He had every reason to be proud of his ancestry, but he elected to speak not from a position of inherited authority but from a position of authority born of experience.

What is known today about the background of William Gilmore Simms is largely owing to the combined and concerted efforts of Simms descendants and Simms scholars struggling to connect the dots between his public and personal life. Born in Charleston on 17 April 1806, William Gilmore Simms could claim freedom fighters on both the paternal and maternal sides of his family. It is therefore worth noting the way Simms responded in 1839 when his friend James Lawson asked about his personal career: "There is little in it that would be interesting to any reader, unless it be such portions of it, as a sense of delicacy would forbid me at present to reveal," he asserted in much the same manner he tactfully declined to reveal the whole of his personal history in years to come. He then proceeded to supply only those details he chose to reveal: "My family was a good one—the paternal side from Ireland, the maternal from Virginia. They were Singletons. My mother's parents removed to Carolina long before the Revolution. All of them took a distinct part on the patriotic side in the struggle with the mother country."[47] While he continued to elaborate on his mother's family and on their many contributions to the cause for freedom, Simms neither mentioned his father's family nor gave to his father any history prior to that acquired in Charleston. Even his father's years in Charleston are left deliberately vague: "My father was unfortunate in business," says absolutely nothing about the senior Simms as a merchant on King Street, successful enough to have owned real estate in Charleston as well as 549 acres of land in the Edgefield District when he left Charleston for the Southwest. As he did for the rest of his life, Simms limited his formally recorded history of his father and elected to focus on the elder Simms as the courageous soldier he no doubt was in fighting under the leadership of Andrew Jackson in the war against the Creek and Seminole Indians and in the Battle of New Orleans. Simms scholars have labored for decades to fill in the many gaps the author left in his father's story.

It has long been known that the elder Simms emigrated from the seaport town of Larne, near Belfast, Ireland, after the War for American Independence. The young man's brothers Matthew and Eli settled in Tennessee. A third brother, James, settled in the Lancaster District of South Carolina. A more recent discovery made by James Everett Kibler has shed new light on the family's Irish roots: "The extended Simms family of merchants in Belfast had gotten into trouble as supporters of the Irish freedom movement. Richard Simms, merchant kinsman and editor of a pro-liberation newspaper in Belfast, had in fact been banished from the country by English authorities."[48] In view of the many readers Simms had accumulated in England, having freedom-fighting Irish ancestors was not information Simms would have wanted to publicize. These Irish ancestors do, however, account for Simms's unflinching courage in editing the *Columbia Phoenix* and in his life-long dedication to freedom.

Because the similarities between Charleston's experience of the War for American Independence and Columbia's experience of the War for Southern Independence are too numerous to be dismissed, it will be useful to note the early impact war in America had on William Gilmore Simms.

He was born one generation after the British evacuation of Charleston. His maternal grandfather John Singleton, had died in 1799. His maternal grandmother, Jane Miller Singleton Gates, was still alive, as was his maternal great-grandfather Thomas Singleton. These two relatives had lived through the invasion and occupation of Charleston by British troops during the seven-year war.

In *Charleston: The Place and the People* (1929) Mrs. St. Julien Ravenel described the young Jane Miller as "strong and fearless" in rowing secret agents across the Ashley River at night during the American Revolution. In discussing Simms's great-grandfather, the wealthy Charleston merchant, tobacco planter, and landowner Thomas Singleton, Ravenel asserted that he "lost a great part of his fortune by lending it to the government for revolutionary purposes" and by being repaid in "depreciated currency." Singleton's home on Church Street was frequently used as a "meeting place for the rebels."[49]

Kinloch Rivers, a great-grandson of William Gilmore Simms, gave a talk in 1987 at Anderson College's Celebration of Carolina Writers, during which he spoke of Thomas Singleton's monkey:

> Singleton had a menagerie in the basement of his house. Among the animals was a pet baboon that he named Balfour after the commander of the British troops that were occupying Charleston. He would dress the baboon in a British uniform and say, "Strut, Balfour, strut." I don't know if the British got wind of this or if it was Singleton's activities on behalf of the patriots, but Singleton got shipped off to St. Augustine as one of the hostages the British took from Charleston.[50]

Before Thomas Singleton was sent to St. Augustine in August of 1780, his son John Singleton married Jane Miller in 1779. John was a captain in command of a detachment under Francis Marion. His brothers, Bracey and Ripley, were part of a company of foot soldiers formed in Charleston on 16 August 1775. They, too, served under Marion during the war against the British. Jane's father, John Miller, from Camden District, South Carolina, was helping to man the fortifications of Charleston in 1780. Captain Miller later died of wounds received during the Battle of Hanging Rock in South Carolina. Born in 1784, the only child of John and Jane Miller Singleton was Harriet Ann Augusta Singleton, who became the wife of William Gilmore Simms Sr. in 1804. Harriet's father had been dead five years. Her widowed mother had become Mrs. Jacob Gates in 1800.

The elder Simms and Mrs. Gates, both of whom died about the same time in early 1831, were actually much closer in age than were the elder Simms and his new twenty-year-old bride, who was twenty-two years younger than he. Despite the difference in their ages, the couple was happy and became the proud parents of a first son, John Singleton Simms, in 1805. The new father had likely followed the progress of the French Revolution to its conclusion. He was no doubt aware of Napoleon's rise to emperor in 1804. As a resident and merchant of a major seaport city, he would have paid particular attention when, after a short interval of peace in Europe, the British and the French renewed their fierce naval warfare in 1804. With both nations harassing neutral ships, American trade was suffering as a consequence.

On 18 April 1806, the day after Simms Jr. was born, Congress passed the Non-Importation Act, which banned the entry into the United States of specific British goods. In October, six months later, the Simmses' first son, John, died. On 22 December 1807, Congress passed the Embargo Act, whereby all foreign trade into or out of the United States was prohibited, and U.S. ships were restricted to coastal trade. As a result, money ceased to circulate among the citizens of Charleston, and business came to a virtual standstill. One month later, on 29 January 1808, Harriet died giving birth to her third son, James, who also died on that date.

In two short years the elder Simms had lost a wife, two sons, and his business. He responded by leaving his surviving child in Charleston with Jane Gates and traveling to Tennessee, a state his brothers Matthew and Eli had elected to consider their home, as had Andrew Jackson long before them.

When the War of 1812 broke out, Jackson was named major general of volunteers. Unlike soldiers in the Continental Army, the volunteers received no pay for the services they rendered to their country—a point the younger Simms repeatedly made many years later. Even so, the elder Simms became a volunteer. He joined John Coffee's celebrated brigade of mounted men in Tennessee.

When Jackson took command of the Creek War on 7 October 1813, he was in charge of Coffee's brigade. At the Battle of Horseshoe Bend in the Mississippi Territory on 27 March 1814, the Tennessee Militia led by General Jackson destroyed the resistance of the Creeks and their Cherokee allies. On 22 May 1814, Jackson was promoted to major general in the U.S. Army and was placed in command of military activities in the South. His campaign against the Creeks ended on 9 August 1814, when they gave all the land they claimed, more than 20 million acres, to the United States. On 7 November 1814, Jackson invaded Spanish Florida and captured Pensacola. Throughout December he was grouping his forces around New Orleans, where from 23 to 31 December he staged a furious stalling action that served to stop the British advance until he could complete his fortifications and breastworks. On 1 January 1815, Jackson's men found themselves in a heavy artillery duel with British troops. They won, only to find themselves having to defend New Orleans against three savage frontal attacks launched by the British from 8 to 27 January 1815. On the final day of battle the defeated British left the field of battle and returned to their ships. British casualties totaled more than two thousand while Jackson's killed and wounded men totaled about seventy. Jackson emerged at the end of the hostilities as the greatest hero of the War of 1812. More significant to the study of Simms as editor of the *Columbia Phoenix* is the fact that the elder Simms had followed Jackson from the beginning of the war to its conclusion.

Great as the Singletons' services to their country had been in the War for American Independence, they had all been rendered long before young Simms was born. The services rendered by Simms's father came at a time when his son was old enough to understand some of their importance. When he started to versify war events at the age of eight or nine, he was writing juvenile poetry about a war in which his father was actually participating under the command of that war's greatest hero. Letters from his father may have been infrequent, but their vivid details stayed with the younger Simms throughout his life. In his talk, Kinloch Rivers confessed, "The story that fascinated and appalled me as a child was that he (the elder Simms) had gone a week with nothing to eat but the meat from his dead horse."[51] Rivers's great-grandfather William Gilmore Simms may well have remembered the story when he reported on South Carolina's starving people and dead horses after Sherman left the state.

In his "Personal Memorabilia," written about 1864, Simms said of his father, "He was a large, admirably formed man, who in his vigor, was over 6 feet in height." Elsewhere in the same work he described his father as being "clever at repartee" and as having "large enthusiasm," "freedom of language," and "great force." Of his father's visit to South Carolina when Simms was twelve years old, he said, "It was then that I knew him first. He was tender and affectionate." The paragraph concludes with Simms recalling, "He impressed me wonderfully with reverence, to which, indeed, I had been inclined from frequent hearing of him."[52]

Because Simms wrote war poetry in his youth, made a lifelong study of war, and considered himself above all else a poet until the day he died, it is appropriate to consider an earlier time when war poetry was employed not as an outpouring of passion onto a printed page but as part of an oral tradition that spread news and kept alive the memories of heroes who displayed valor in combat. The earliest war poets were not only expected to observe and to record the events of battle but also to participate in struggles right up to the end. They took their places behind the shield walls that served to protect them so long as they held. They were then excused from fighting to the death so that they could tell the stories and increase the glory of those heroes who either won or lost the battles.

Celtic war poets used gritty and muscular language not unlike what Simms occasionally used in his more powerful war poems. As war poetry evolved from the spreading of news and the recording of events and the recounting of history, to the recording of emotions of soldiers during wartimes, it took on a more romantic language. Over time war poetry advanced to include causes of war, the cost of war to those who experienced it, and the rousing martial lyrics that inspired patriotism and called young men to fight.

Simms was aware that novels had superseded poems as the dominant literary form. Newspapers were spreading news to those who were living in war zones. Still a good bit of his newspaper account of Columbia's destruction reads like a prose poem. It is fast-paced, action-packed, and filled with details. It also has touches of humor. Like physicians, soldiers and civilians living in theaters of conflict see much death and suffering and must employ a healthy dose of comedy to lighten the burden in order to endure. The elderly and disabled, the old men and women and children of Columbia had to assume the courage and resolve of soldiers. They were witnessing the devastation of their property, their city, and their country by an invading army.

A voracious reader as a youth, Simms had by age twelve begun a study of medicine, obtained through the *Materia Medica*. He began his apprenticeship in a local pharmacist's shop. Six years spent in preparing and selling medicines not only opened his eyes to a previously unimagined realm of human suffering but also served to convince the budding author that his true calling lay in another field.

It is doubtful the grandmother raising him and the father keeping track of him from a distance ever let him lose sight of his need to prepare himself for a proper profession. Neither would have encouraged his becoming an author unless he could support himself. And so, at eighteen, Simms transitioned from medicine to law. What he took from his apprenticeship was a well developed compassion for others, an empathy that can be seen in his editing of the *Columbia Phoenix*. He had been brought into contact with a wide variety of people, had learned to listen carefully, to observe closely, and to retain mentally what he had heard and seen. These traits also served him well in recounting the sack and destruction of his state capital. Although his account is not written in the style of a legal brief, it does contain material a lawyer would need to argue in a court of law, and it also reflects a working knowledge of what would and would not constitute war crimes.

Simms studied law in the office of Charles R. Carroll, a family friend who like the Simmses was also from an immigrant family of Northern Ireland. Having become a published poet in the Charleston newspapers at the age of sixteen, Simms continued to write while he trained for the legal profession in much the same way he had written throughout most of his apprenticeship in the pharmacist's shop. At the age of nineteen he was one year into his study of law when he had his first book of poetry published, *Monody, on the Death of Gen. Charles Cotesworth Pinckney* (1825).

Simms traveled in 1825 through the Indian territory west of the Mississippi with his father and his Uncle James. His father, who had finally settled in Mississippi after the Battle of New Orleans, had been trying unsuccessfully for the better part of ten years to convince his son to join him there. In 1824 the younger Simms had visited the elder's plantation on the Pearl River, near Columbia, Mississippi, for the first time. Neither the 1824 nor the 1825 visit could lure young Gilmore Simms from his Charleston home. After each trip, he returned to Charleston to his law studies and to his childhood sweetheart, Anna Malcolm Giles.

He married Anna in 1826. In 1827 their only child, Anna Augusta Singleton Simms, was born, and Simms was admitted to the bar on his twenty-first birthday. Fatherhood and law practice did not deter Simms the poet, who published two collections of verse, *Lyrical and Other Poems* and *Early Lays*, before the end of 1827.

Soon appointed a magistrate for Charleston, Simms continued to shift his attention back and forth for several years between law and literature. By the time he finally left the law for a literary career, his written work was reflecting his legal training. It continued to do so for the rest of his life.

Simms, who never lost interest in medicine or law, rapidly acquired influential friends in both the medical and the legal fields. Experience as a trial lawyer had given him confidence and an air of authority as a public speaker, leading to public orations so powerfully delivered that they in turn opened doors to new opportunities and new associates.

By age twenty-four, he had published five volumes of poetry, which had been warmly received and duly praised in his hometown. His poetry had found favor with Bryant, and Simms's youthful editorial career, first with the *Southern Literary Gazette* in 1828–1829 and next with the *Charleston City Gazette* in 1830–1832, had provided him with literary contacts in the North.

Simms's many accomplishments and influential friends could not lift his spirits when Anna died of tuberculosis on 19 February 1832. At twenty-six he became the single parent of a four-year-old daughter. His father and maternal grandmother, Jane Singleton Gates, had died within a month of each other in 1831. Anna's death renewed and compounded the young author's grief. Complete responsibility for his only child's welfare weighed on his heart.

In pain and frustration he traveled North for the first time with a batch of unpublished manuscripts and spent the summer of 1832 making literary friends and preparing his sixth volume of poetry for publication. James Lawson agreed to see *Atalantis: A Story of the Sea* through the press of the Harper brothers, who had also become friends of Simms. By year's end the success of *Atalantis* had brought Simms to the attention of both the American press and the British press.

Out of his personal loss had come a professional triumph; he had made a name for himself. As he ventured from poetry into novels, Simms became not only famous but also one of the first professional authors in America to make a modest living solely through his writing. Spending summers in the North, where he conducted much of the business of his literary career, became routine. He spent the rest of the year in South Carolina, where he drew inspiration and composed his works for publication.

Fame and modest fortune did not render Simms immune to disappointments and tragedies. His marriage to Chevillette Roach in 1836 produced fifteen children; only his first child, by Anna, and five of his children by Chevillette lived to maturity. He was elected to the South Carolina House of Representatives and served from 1844 to 1846, only to be defeated by a slight majority in the race for lieutenant governor in 1846. The defeat left its mark. Nominated in the Charleston papers for Congress in 1850, Simms declined the nomination. Urged by James Henry Hammond to become a candidate in 1858 for the U.S. Senate, Simms again declined.

The Confederate War had just begun when Simms's Charleston townhouse on Smith Street burned. He suffered the loss of a ninth child shortly thereafter. In 1862 Woodlands burned. Despite the war, the people of South Carolina collected enough money to have it rebuilt. In 1863 Simms received the most crushing blow of all. Chevillette, his wife for twenty-seven years, died suddenly of acute appendicitis. Friends feared he would lose his sanity, so deep was his distress. His twenty-year-old son, Gilmore, was at the time a Confederate soldier fighting at the front. His oldest daughter, Augusta, was married and living in Charleston when Chevillette died at Woodlands. Simms had with him at Woodlands two daughters, aged sixteen and thirteen, one son aged seven, and a baby boy not yet a year old. In 1864 Gilmore was wounded in battle in Virginia, lost a finger, recovered in South Carolina, and returned to duty. In January of 1865 Augusta's second child and Simms's first grandson, Simms, died at the age of four.

With Sherman's troops coming closer, Simms—whose trips to Columbia had grown more frequent throughout the war—sought shelter in the capital city for his family. When Sherman entered Columbia on 17 February 1865, all Simms's surviving children except Gilmore, who was still serving in the Confederate army, were in the city with him, as was his only surviving grandchild, Augusta's six-year-old daughter, Chevillette. The place Simms felt would be the safest had become instead the most dangerous. The invasion of South Carolina and the capture of Columbia brought a level of destruction few South Carolinians could have ever imagined.

When he took to the streets of Columbia to observe Sherman's troops in action, Simms had no way of knowing Woodlands had already been torched by stragglers following in the wake of the main army. He later wrote to Judge Benjamin Perry on 6 March 1865, "The humbleness and obscurity of our abode, constituted its security. It held forth too little promise to the plunderers, and so escaped the fire."[53] The Simms family of seven was then sharing two rooms in a house in Columbia. This humble abode was the home of George E. Isaacs and his wife, Rebecca M. Giles Isaacs, who was a relative of Simms's first wife, Anna Malcolm Giles. The Isaacs had three daughters.

Some of Simms's friends of longstanding were scattered throughout the city. Mrs. Louisa McCord, whose literary career had been championed by Simms from its beginning, was in her Columbia home on the corner of Pendleton and Bull streets. Until the last possible minute, Mrs. Mary Boykin Chesnut was living in a cottage on Hampton Street, rented by her husband, James Chesnut, from Dr. John Julian Chisolm, who was then stationed in Charleston. Mary Boykin Chesnut was the daughter of Stephen Decatur Miller, once the governor of South Carolina. Her husband had served as aide to General Pierre Gustave Toutant Beauregard, then as aide to President Jefferson Davis before being appointed a brigadier general commanding the reserves in South Carolina. When in mid February Mary Chesnut fled to North Carolina, Louisa McCord considered sending her daughters along to provide for their safety. Instead she positioned the girls in the upstairs portion of the house and had the staircase removed. There they remained during the four days General O. O. Howard and his staff occupied the widow's home, which they ransacked, littering the yard with her personal papers before they left.

Henry Timrod was another close friend of Simms. Like Louisa McCord, Timrod was a native Charlestonian living in Columbia when Sherman approached the city. As a war correspondent for the *Mercury*, Timrod had traveled to Mississippi to cover General Beauregard's troops in Corinth after the Battle of Shiloh. By the time he returned to his sister Emily's home in Columbia, Timrod was being called "Poet Laureate of the Confederate South." In 1863 Dr. Robert W. Gibbes sold the *Daily South Carolinian* of Columbia to Felix Gregory De Fontaine. On 12 January 1864, Timrod had joined the staff of the paper as associate editor with a part ownership. De Fontaine was editor, and Julian Selby, who had been with the paper for twenty years, ran the press. Both owned greater shares than Timrod. On 16 February 1864, Timrod married Katie Goodwin, the sister of George Goodwin, who was the husband of Timrod's sister Emily.

One year later Timrod was the father of a newborn son; his brother-in-law was dead; his mother and sisters were living in Columbia, and De Fontaine had taken most of the paper's newsprint and supplies to the upper part of the state as Sherman advanced on the city. Timrod and Selby remained in Columbia, as did Gibbes.

All were located within walking distance of one another, although Timrod was forced to keep himself concealed while Sherman's troops occupied the city. Years of writing poetry, political commentary, and editorials supportive of the South and critical of the invading Northern armies, in addition to making statements mocking Sherman, had rendered the new father a target for Federal vengeance at the very time his tuberculosis was becoming more pronounced.

While Simms could not be everywhere at once during Columbia's destruction, he knew distinguished and reliable sources throughout the city, many of them for more than thirty years. Louisa McCord, Mary Boykin Chesnut, Henry Timrod, Dr. Robert W. Gibbes, Felix De Fontaine, and Julian Selby were only some of the large number of people to whom Simms had ready access. These people could report to Simms not only their own experiences but also what they had heard about the sufferings of others. Foreign correspondents might have to search for eyewitness observers, but Simms was able to report his personal observations as well as the accounts of people in his wide circle of acquaintances.

Had Simms delayed in accumulating eyewitness accounts, his story of Columbia's destruction would have been different. People left the city in numbers impossible to determine. Some returned to the districts from which they had fled. Some relocated to distant regions where family or friends opened their homes. Others simply started their lives over in the first suitable place they could find. Locating witnesses at a later date would have presented substantial problems.

Some of the witnesses died. Some became disabled. Already sick or elderly citizens facing starvation, exposure to the elements, inadequate clothing, lack of medical care, and the threat of infection while in weakened physical states had an increased likelihood of dying after the invasion. Pregnant women, especially women going into labor or premature labor, and women exhausted by recent childbirth were also at risk. All these people had stories they might not live to tell. The greatest problem, though, for a reporter or historian is fear. Approached soon after a crisis, many witnesses are almost relieved to relate their hardships, but as time passes, these same people begin to take into account the long-term consequences of telling what they know to be true. They consider their own circumstances, and those of the people they love, and become fearful that they could jeopardize their safety by speaking out. If life, home, property, family, or reputations are threatened, then witnesses might not lie, but they could refrain from telling either the truth or the whole truth.

When Union troops re-entered Columbia on 25 May 1865, arrested the governor, and garrisoned the city, the number of survivors willing to speak openly about the destruction of their city no doubt dropped considerably. From that day to this, no other reporter, historian or author, could equal Simms's account. Time-altered perceptions, testimonies tainted by self-interest or self-protection, missing witnesses, and the absence of physical evidence did not present the obstacles to Simms they presented to future writers. The wisdom and life experience of an author nearing sixty years of age—in addition to Simms's knowledge of medical, legal, historical, and literary matters—equipped him well for the document he set out to write. "The Capture, Sack, and Destruction of the City of Columbia" is a little-known masterpiece in American life and literature.

IV.

The Columbia Phoenix

The diary kept by Emma LeConte, seventeen-year-old daughter of Professor Joseph LeConte, contains information helpful in accessing the conditions of the people for whom the *Columbia Phoenix* was published. Written from 31 December 1864 to 10 August 1865 in her Columbia home on the campus of South Carolina College, *When the World Ended: The Diary of Emma LeConte* clearly establishes the desires of the people in Columbia for news during this period of major crisis.

Signs of traumatic stress and posttraumatic-stress syndrome are revealed in words such as *hysteria*, *anxiety*, and *depression*, which are scattered among Emma's accounts of sleeplessness, inability to eat, loss of focus, lack of interest in daily routines, exhaustion, mood swings, and lethargy. Shifts from optimism to extreme rage to utter hopelessness are frequent.

Since Emma wrote much of her diary after Sherman's troops had left the city, in a house that had been neither burned nor plundered, we may safely assume that residents who had experienced the double traumas of fire and theft were suffering symptoms even greater than Emma's. She reported "wandering aimlessly about the house" and "sitting listless in the sun." When she tried to read, she found, "I did not know what I was reading." Then she asserted, "I suppose it is the reaction from the frightful strain and nervous tension."[54]

On 18 March 1865, almost a month after the destruction of Columbia, Emma wrote a lengthy entry in her diary that is significant not only because it mentions the *Columbia Phoenix* by name just days before the appearance of its first issue, but also because it clearly demonstrates the community's need for a reliable editor and a dependable newspaper to combat the thousands of rumors spreading throughout the city. The telegraph lines were down. Slaughtered horses and destroyed carriages had turned Columbians into pedestrians at a time when walking on streets or sidewalks could be dangerous. Friends and family members were searching for one another. The homeless were seeking shelter. The hungry were looking for food. And Emma was recording details being brought into the city while she anxiously awaited the return of her father, who had ventured as far as Augusta in search of provisions.

She rejoiced when some people "found their way on foot to Columbia" because they brought "tidings from Charleston." She recorded the experiences of "a Mr. Middleton, eighty years old," who joined his family in the capital after being "ordered by ruffians to leave his house." He had "watched his burning house till it was consumed and then, taking the road to Columbia, walked the entire distance from Georgetown." She apparently knew Mr. Pope, who "has just got in," having escaped the Yankees "by passing himself off as a preacher."

Emma did not record where Mr. Pope had come from or where he was when he encountered Yankees boasting of having burned Columbia: "On his inquiring the cause of the conflagration, they at first repeated the story of the whiskey, but one fellow said frankly that he might as well tell the truth—that Sherman had ordered them to burn it, that they had expected to burn it, and they *did* burn the hole of secession."[55] Being one of only about seven thousand people left in Columbia after its destruction, Emma was no doubt curious as to what its invaders had to say regarding the city's destruction.

Still essentially cut off from the outside world, Columbians were hearing "many wild and dreadful rumors." Mrs. Bird, passing through "on her way from Richmond to Augusta" told of Richmond's prevailing "despondency." But Emma noted, "We know almost nothing—the only reliable news from couriers and they come so rarely." She also admitted, "Every scrap of news or even rumor from the entire world is seized upon in this forlorn town."[56]

Near the end of her last entry prior to 1 April 1865, she inserted the only sentence that ends with an exclamation: "We are also soon to have a tri-weekly paper edited by Gilmer Sims and called 'The Phoenix'!"[57] Although Emma misspelled his name, William Gilmore Simms was indeed known to many in his state simply as Gilmore Simms. The newspaper did begin as a triweekly, and it is interesting that Emma not only placed the editor's name before that of the paper but also failed to mention the name of its publisher or the name of anyone else associated with the *Phoenix*. This sentence, which follows a report that "Telegraphic communications will be opened with Richmond in a few days,"[58] may indicate that the editor and publisher were holding the press until a return of telegraph service made back-and-forth news transmissions possible.

The Simms name was obviously important to the intelligent and educated Emma LeConte. Equally obvious is the great responsibility Simms was assuming as editor of a paper established to assist in the rebuilding of Columbia: "We trust that the advent of *The Columbia Phoenix* will prove . . . favorable to the resuscitation of our brave old city from her ashes. We must not sit and wring our hands idly, but go at once to our duties. . . . Like the Phoenix, our city shall spring from her ashes."[59]

Simms was not confining his efforts to the rebuilding of streets, houses, gardens, and public structures. He was also determined to rebuild the hope, the courage, and the determination of his people, to reinstill in them the spirit of creating a new civilization with energy and vigor, just as South Carolinians had done after the British evacuation of Charleston at the end of the War for American Independence. Remembering the energy and vigor of older generations of Southerners, Simms wrote an editorial statement insisting "we are really in the condition of a people just beginning to colonize in a strange land, whose resources we do not know."[60]

An important analysis of the *Columbia Phoenix* during the six months it was edited by Simms has been written by James Everett Kibler, who noted its "broken type, uneven margins and coarse paper" as well as its striking resemblance to "colonial gazettes." Kibler also identified Simms as the contributor of "most of the original matter" especially that emphasizing "courage and endurance in a time of trial." In referring to essays written by Simms, Kibler focused particular attention on one "noteworthy from a journalistic standpoint," which "states that public opinion, which governs a democracy, can be manipulated for good or ill by the press." Simms vowed that the *Phoenix* would offer diversified opinions and supply selections from northern papers. As Kibler noted, Simms "was aware of the propagandistic distortion of the South in the northern press and vowed that the reverse would not occur in the *Phoenix*." Because selections from northern papers were included "most frequently without commentary," the reader was left free "to make up his own mind."[61]

Simms, accustomed to expressing his opinions freely, wrote scathing criticisms of the activities of Northern occupation forces once they were established in Columbia in late May of 1865. Julian Selby, as publisher of the *Phoenix*, probably feared with good reason that Simms would get both of them arrested and sometimes suggested "a little toning down of his articles," but to little avail. When the expected article of arrest was made out near the end of June, only the editor was arrested by Federal soldiers. According to Selby, "a corporal and squad of soldiers" escorted Simms "before the offended General, at his headquarters" where "military law was being dispensed." Because Simms was "well advanced in years," he was permitted to sit down,

> directly in front of the General, and the trial began. In a very short time the charge was dismissed, and Mr. S. was invited to partake of an elegant luncheon in an adjoining room, which he politely accepted. When Mr. Simms returned to his quarters, it was in Gen. Hartwell's carriage, with a large basket filled with champagne and canned delicacies. The General expressed himself . . . the next day, to the effect that if Mr. S. was a specimen of the

South Carolina gentleman, he would never enter into a tilt with one of them again. "He out-talked me, out-drank me, and very clearly and politely showed me that I lacked proper respect for the aged." Col. Haughton heard the General out and replied simply, "I told you so."[62]

Haughton's response is not surprising, since Selby also says the officers were great admirers of Simms and that two or three of them dropped by daily to chat with him. Nor is it surprising Simms continued to write articles such as "Thieving as One of the Fine Arts," in which the occupying military government remained a target.

The first issue of the *Columbia Phoenix* came out on 21 March 1865 and was sold door to door. Published on Tuesdays, Thursdays, and Saturdays, it remained a triweekly until 10 April 1865, when it became a daily newspaper. On 15 May 1865 its title became the *Columbia Daily Phoenix*. On 31 July 1865 the title was changed to the *Daily Phoenix*. No subscriptions were taken until after the ninth issue, when people could subscribe on a daily basis for twenty dollars a month or on a triweekly basis for ten dollars a month. Either way payment was due in advance.

An important feature of the newspaper's first issue was a mission statement focused on hope, prayer, and Divine Providence:

> We, this day, present to our readers the first number of a newspaper. We trust that the advent of the Columbia *Phoenix* will prove an augury favorable to the resuscitation of our brave old city from her ashes. We are full of hope ourselves, and trust that our people will share the hope with us. We must not despond, but let our citizens, rising, with heart and faith firmly fixed on that Divine Providence which suffers no sparrow to fall unnoticed to the ground, proceed to their labors manfully, each in his vocation, and all working together, until our city is renovated, renewed, regenerated, and springs, with all her temples and palaces, her shrines of art and industry, into a strength and splendor superior even to the past. We must not sit and wring our hands idly, but go at once to our duties. The toil alone, honestly pursued, will heal all the hurts of fortune. Be of good cheer, brethren—each having faith in the other and all in God, and let us work out our deliverance like men. There is no lane so long that it hath no turning—no fortune so tenacious of its ill aspect as will not smile at last upon the confiding faith which labors and prays together. Like the *Phoenix*, our city shall spring from her ashes, and *our Phoenix*, we hope and trust, shall announce the glorious rising! God save the State!

The mission statement was followed by a brief review of the newspaper's birth pains and blessings:

On the Tramp: We have had a terrible time of toil and weariness in our tramp after a press and type and paper. Such roads, such a route, such mud, such water, such clay and bitter weather. But through the blessings of the good God, we have succeeded, and the result is before our pleasant public. We own much to the good friends who cheered us and helped us along the road. Verily, we found many Samaritans, who never felt the itch of gain so keenly as to sacrifice humanity for the sake of Mammon. Everywhere did they receive the footsore pilgrim with hospitality. They spread the board and the bed with willing kindness; killed for us the fatted lamb, and set the wheaten loaf upon the table, and in but a single instance would any one receive a single copper in compensation from the wallet of the wayfarer. And ours was the experience of many along the route from Columbia to Newberry, from Newberry to Abbeville, and from Abbeville to Greenville. We shall long remember the patriarchal kindness of Mr. J. S. Bowers and several other gentlemen connected with the Greenville Railroad; Col S. Fair, Messrs. M. Barr and R. Greneker, of Newberry; Mrs. Dr. Service, Mrs. John Sassard, Mrs. Wier, Messrs. Hugh Wilson and Wm. Moore, of Abbeville; Messrs. J. S. Bailey and G. W. Huff, of Greenville.

Although future issues of the newspaper were sold door to door for one dollar, it was necessary to charge double this amount for the first.

The *Phoenix.*—Our *Phoenix* does not rise from the flames and ashes without great cost and effort. We have toiled laboriously and expended much money in enabling her to clothe herself in new plumage and to soar. These labors and this cost will be cheerfully shared, we doubt not, by our fellow citizens. We shall be constrained to charge somewhat more highly at first for our *Phoenix* than we expect to do hereafter. After the few first numbers of our paper, which require of us extra expenditure of money, we shall endeavor to accommodate our charges to the usual standard of our contemporaries. The price of the first number will be $2.

A tribute to the generosity of neighbors was also placed in the first issue of the newspaper.

THE SAMARITAN CITIES AND PEOPLE.—The citizens of Columbia owe an eternal debt of gratitude to the noble generosity of the people of Augusta, Charlotte, Chester, Newberry, Abbeville, Greenville, Sumter and other places, for the promptness and wonderful liberality which came to their relief and rescue at the hour of their worst tribulation. We were starving and they brought us food, naked and they gave us clothing, sorrowing and they poured into our souls the words of comfort, encouragement and sympathy. Nor should we forget the Samaritan love of these people of Charlotte and other towns who welcomed our fugitives to their homes and firesides. We shall not forget them, and it is grateful to know that if God sends us the storm, He guides us to the shelter; if He afflicts us with the scourge, He finds the remedy; if He tests our hearts with trial, He strengthens us with faith until hope is renewed within us.

While one of the main purposes of the *Phoenix* was to help in the rebuilding of Columbia, the newspaper also served as a suitable vehicle for the publication of Simms's great record of the burning of Columbia. Simms's "The Capture, Sack, and Destruction of the City of Columbia" was serialized over a three-week period, which began with the paper's first issue on 21 March 1865 and ended with its issue of 10 April 1865. Simms later revised, shortened, and somewhat toned down the work as a separate publication, which the Daily Phoenix Press published in October 1865 as a soft-bound pamphlet. Like the legendary phoenix bird, which after several centuries of life consumed itself in fire and then rose from its ashes in youthful freshness, Columbia—along with Simms's accounts of her sufferings—would survive and finally reappear.

Several observations must be made pertaining to "The Capture, Sack, and Destruction of the City of Columbia" as it originally appeared in newspaper form. The purpose of Simms's account was to provide the public with news accurately detailed and honestly reported, based on visible evidence as well as on fairly conducted interviews. With telegraph operations re-established, the newspaper account could be transmitted to a wider audience of interested readers beyond the environs of Columbia. Even if Simms had intended from the first to republish the account in book form, waiting to do so would have negated its immediate value as news that the public needed to know and wanted to hear.

A second purpose closely linked to the account's timeliness as news was the dated documentation of facts pertaining to loss of property, constituting grounds for complaints in a court of law. A close inspection of the account from its opening statements to its carefully constructed summation calls to mind the years Simms spent in the legal field. As a lawyer who had presented cases in court, Simms would have known the value of eyewitness accounts, the importance of obtaining facts while they were still fresh in the minds of witnesses and the way such accounts diminished in value with the passing of time.

A third purpose was the documentation of significant historical information. By 1865 Simms had read and written enough history to feel obligated to record a firsthand account that could serve as primary source material for a critical period he recognized as a turning point in his state's history and in the history of America, not to mention the history of warfare.

Another purpose—and perhaps the most important—was to unite the people of the South and of South Carolina in their suffering and their belief in Divine

Providence. Unless Simms's account is viewed in this light, the first two sentences make little sense: "It has pleased God, in that Providence which is so inscrutable to man, to visit our beautiful city with the most cruel fate which can ever befall States or cities. He has permitted the cruel and malignant enemy to penetrate our country almost without impediment; to pollute our homes with his presence; to rob and ravage our dwellings, and to commit three-fifths of our city to the flames."

Simms might as well have told his readers he was preparing a modern version of the Book of Job, and for much the same reason Job's story had been recorded in the first place. Long considered one of the literary masterpieces of the world, the Book of Job is a dramatic poem of ancient wisdom often interpreted as a book that deals with the suffering of the innocent and the problems of justice and retribution. As a poet, as a student of literature and the Bible, Simms perceived analogies between Job and his friends, on one hand, and between the people of Columbia in their reversal of fortune and critics who loudly insisted the plight of South Carolinians was just punishment from God for wrongdoing.

Simms was writing at a time when many Northerners dismissed the destruction of Columbia as just retribution. Simms's response was to frame his account of what his state and home had suffered in the context of the ancient wise man's record of his sufferings and endurance. Simms concluded, "It is for us, as succinctly but as fully as possible, and in the simplest language, to endeavor to make the melancholy record of our wretchedness, so that our sons may always remember, and the whole Christian world everywhere may read." Echoing Job, who in his humiliation covered himself in ashes, Simms wrote, "Humiliation spreads her ashes on our homes and garments." Invasion of his land, theft of his property, and illness were part of Job's story, just as invasion, theft and wanton destruction of property, and physical affliction of the people had become the primary story of Columbia. The parallels were understood. Simms's account became more than a melancholy record. It was a source of hope and guidance and promise, notwithstanding the counsel of false friends or the false records of self-serving critics. Just as Job's sufferings resulted in a deeper experience of God and a stronger faith in life, so the sufferings of the people of Columbia—Simms proclaimed—would lead to greater awareness and to a larger humanity. By enduring the North's wanton invasion, the people of the South would forever be united in their memories of a shared suffering, which included cruel and unjust treatment.

Appearing in the *Phoenix* as "The Capture, Sack, and Destruction of the City of Columbia" and in pamphlet form as *Sack and Destruction of the City of Columbia, S.C.*, Simms's description did much to affect his name in the public record. Books by Sherman's men justifying the invasion and excusing the burning of

Columbia came swiftly into the marketplace; most mentioned Simms and his Woodlands Plantation, depicting him and his eyewitness account in less than complimentary terms.

One of the first books to glorify Sherman's conduct during the invasion of the South was written by Sherman's aide-de-camp, Major George Ward Nichols. In *The Story of the Great March* (1865) Nichols asserted, "In the record of great wars we read of vast armies marching through an enemy's country, carrying death and destruction in their path; of villages burned, cities pillaged, tribe or nation swept out of existence." Alexander's conquering legions, the armies of the Romans, and the warriors of the Gauls were all mentioned before Nichols made his point: "History, however, will be searched in vain for a parallel to the scathing and destructive effects of the Invasion of the Carolinas. The immediate disasters to the Rebel cause, the cities captured, arsenals and munitions of war destroyed, the communications severed, will be appreciated by the military mind in Europe, as well as by our own army and people."[63]

Nichols may have been ignorant of the laws of war. He may not have known why Napoleon was both punished and banished from Europe after twenty years of aggressive warfare. Perhaps he did not know what constituted a war crime. But graduates of West Point knew all these things. Sherman acknowledged as much in a letter to his friend J. B. Fry years later: "I know that in the beginning I, too, had the old West Point notion that pillage was a capital crime, and punished it by shooting." Apparently Sherman saw other West Point lessons as "notions" since Nichols quoted him as saying, "There is a class of persons at the South who must be exterminated before there can be peace in the land."[64]

To Nichols, Southerners should have had no complaints against invasion and extermination: "If," he said, "the personal descriptions of the General given by the Rebel newspapers during his campaign were accepted as truth, he would appear as a creature of demoniac passion and cruelty, whose unrelenting spirit found pleasure in wreaking vengeance upon old men, women, and children; but Rebel journalism is known to be violent, unscrupulous, and libelous, as readily assailing the President with coarse vituperation as his generals with wholesale falsehood."[65]

While Nichols never mentioned the *Columbia Phoenix* or Simms by name, there is little reason to doubt he was fully aware of Simms's account of the destruction of Columbia and was perhaps attempting to do a little damage control at a time when Sherman's name was being associated with war crimes. Nichols claimed, "General Sherman and his officers worked with their own hands until long after midnight, trying to save life and property."[66] Here Nichols exaggerated since Sherman's memoirs state that he sent Major Nichols to "inquire the cause" of "a bright light shining on the walls" of his bedroom in the

Blanton Duncan house soon after dark and was told "there seemed to be a house on fire down about the market-house." Sherman reported sending "messengers after messengers" to his generals and receiving "repeated assurances that all was being done that could be done." Sherman did not go downtown until "about eleven o'clock at night"[67] and never said, or even implied, that he worked with his own hands until long after midnight. Had he done so, it is likely he would have made the fact known when he was called before the Mixed Claims Commission for questioning.

Nichols repeatedly attempted to absolve Sherman: "Whatever may have been the cause of the disaster, the direful result is deprecated by General Sherman most emphatically; for however heinous the crimes of this people against our common country, we do not war against women and children and helpless persons."[68] How much Sherman deprecated the result is called into question by Nichols's later assertion that "Columbia will have bitter cause to remember the visit of Sherman's army. Even if peace and prosperity soon return to the land, not in this generation or the next—no, not for a century—can this city or the state recover from the deadly blow which has taken its life." He further contended, "I know that thousands of South Carolina's sons are in the army of the rebellion; but she has already lost her best blood there. Those who remain have no homes. The Hamptons, Barnwells, Simses, Rhetts, Singletons, Prestons, have no homes. The ancient homesteads where were gathered sacred associations, the heritages of many generations, are swept away. When first these men became traitors they lost honor; today they have no habitations; in the glorious future of this country they will have no name."[69]

One of the men Nichols predicted would have no future name is Simms, although Nichols misspelled his name and failed to give it earlier when he wrote, "Tonight we are encamped upon the place of one of South Carolina's most high-blooded chivalry—one of those persons who believed himself to have been brought into the world to rule over his fellow-creatures, a sort of Grand Pasha, and all that sort of thing."[70] The place and the date given to this diary entry establishes the campsite in the Barnwell District of Orangeburg at Woodlands Plantation.

Almost twenty years later, F. Y. Hedley of Sherman's army published *Marching through Georgia* (1884), in which he said of Orangeburg, "W. Gilmore Simms, the famous Southern author, had his home at this place. Whether his premises were destroyed or not, the author does not know; but many books from his library, bearing his autograph, found their way into camp, and were carried away by the men as mementoes."[71]

Nichols may have avoided making a direct reference to Simms's account of the destruction of Columbia because Simms was very much alive and surely would have taken the Northern author to task in a very public way. Hedley, however, felt perfectly safe. When his account came out, Simms had been dead fourteen years and so could not dispute Hedley, who started his chapter on Columbia by declaring, "Many accounts have been written about the destruction of Columbia, notably that from the pen of the distinguished Southern author, William Gilmore Simms. This in common with others, is founded upon information acquired at second-hand, and is wide of the truth in many important particulars."[72]

After providing many quotes from Simms's account, Hedley contended, "These are some of the passionate assertions of a bitter partisan, who was not within fifty miles of Columbia at the time of its destruction and whose information is wholly second-hand, and unsupported by evidence."[73] Since Simms had as usual kept his personal and professional lives separate and had not mentioned his family in his account of Columbia's destruction, Hedley had no way of knowing there were members of the Simms family yet alive who could attest to the presence of Simms in Columbia on the night in question. All his daughters and one of his sons in Columbia on that night were then old enough to remember the attack, not only on the city but also on their father.

By mentioning Simms, by quoting his account, and by trying to refute it, Hedley proved how difficult it still was more than fourteen years after the death of South Carolina's best-known antebellum author to erase his name from public memory. Even outside Charleston and South Carolina, Simms's name haunted the men who had invaded the Carolinas. Simms's voice was not easy to silence. Only a concerted effort could reduce its power or the impact of its eyewitness testimony to the horrors of the Northern invasion.

As far back as 1952, Donald Davidson of Vanderbilt University was insisting, "Neglect of an author of Simms' stature is nothing less than a scandal when it results—as it has resulted in his case—in the disappearance of his books from the common market and therefore from the readers' bookshelf. This is literary murder—the slow-working equivalent of the 'burning of the books' now so often and so justly decried."[74] Davidson also compared William P. Trent's 1892 biography of Simms to the sort of thing one would see "if one had in hand a biography of Mary, Queen of Scots, written by John Knox."[75] Davidson was neither the first nor certainly the last literary scholar to complain of Trent's misrepresentations of Simms.

Now that works by Simms are being read and studied in this and other countries, more scholars are embracing Davidson's assessment of Simms's reputation. Mary Ann Wimsatt in her introduction to *Tales of the South by William Gilmore Simms* (1996) mentioned the national popularity Simms enjoyed prior to the War for Southern Independence and the changes that adversely affected his popularity at its conclusion: "For after the war, Northern historians and literary historians, backed by the powerful Northern publishing industry, rewrote American history in a manner fundamentally unsympathetic toward the South and its authors. The prevailing interpretation of the South, which still operates in the late twentieth century, has distorted the national understanding of South-ern culture and literature, particularly of antebellum culture and literature, and most particularly of Simms." Wimsatt also noted, "Happily for people who appreciate Simms's central role in American as well as Southern literature and history, several books that treat the man and his work from enlightened, sympa-thetic perspectives are beginning to diminish ignorance and to alter long-entrenched negative beliefs about the gifted South Carolinian."[76]

Forty-four years separate the observations made by Davidson in 1952 and Wimsatt in 1996. Neither of these literary scholars delved into the issue of reli-gious differences that existed between the North and the South before and after the war. Nor did they mention the perceived unpardonable sin Simms commit-ted when he published an account of Columbia's destruction in which he dared to deny the North a righteous victory in an aggressive war Northerners were determined to view as justifiable.

The issue of religious freedom was not one Simms cared to avoid any more than he avoided the issues of freedom of speech and freedom of the press. Simms begins his account of the destruction of Columbia by alluding to the Book of Job, the ancient story of a righteous man who lost everything he possessed, not through any fault or sin of his own but simply because it was God's pleasure to allow him to suffer: "It has pleased God, in that Providence which is so inscrutable to man, to visit our beautiful city with the most cruel fate which can ever befall States or cities." Job's friends visit him and claim to comfort him but instead argue that no one could suffer as much as he has without being guilty of heinous crimes against mankind and vile sins against God. Job repeatedly declares his innocence; at the conclusion of the book Yahweh reproves Job's friends for their fallacious arguments and arrogant attitudes and then vindicates the innocent sufferer. The Book of Job is commonly read as an attempt to face the philosophical problem of why righteous and innocent people must endure serious suffering. Even though Job's wealth, family, and reputation are restored in the prose epilogue, his greatest victory—most would assert—is that Yahweh reveals himself to Job in the midst of so much agony and suffering.

Furthermore, Simms alluded in his opening paragraph to Thomas Jefferson's Declaration of Independence, which announced that the American colonies were asserting their natural right to secede from Great Britain in order to form their own consensual governmsent. By listing some of the public buildings destroyed by Sherman and his men, Simms led the reader to wonder how

Americans could claim any longer to defend consensual government when their venerable structures of government are destroyed. How can Americans claim to have freedom of religion when their churches are burned? How can Americans claim to have freedom of speech and freedom of the press when printing presses and newspapers are destroyed? How can Americans claim to have inalienable rights to pursue happiness when their homes are plundered and burned? How can Americans enjoy the right to prosper when banking establishments are destroyed? Simms alerted the reader immediately that the cruel and malignant invasion had deprived Southern Americans of the very rights they had fought and died for in the War for American Independence.

Simms concluded his introductory paragraph by stating why he had written this eyewitness account of Columbia's destruction: "good citizens must always remember the burning of Columbia so that such atrocities will never be repeated." This record has been made "so that our sons may always remember and the whole Christian world everywhere may read." These sons of the state may be of any religious affiliation. Simms did not limit them to Christian sons. Nor did Simms divide the Christian world into Roman Catholic and Protestant and Greek Orthodox, nor did he divide Protestants into denominations. He did not limit the Christian readership to any one continent or insist that this Christian readership remember anything specific in what they have read. Rather, Simms was making a distinctly American point: America was founded by people committed to freedom; the founders had overcome religious differences in order to establish a safe haven for people of various faiths; none was expected to wage holy wars by forcing his or her views of God's justice and God's kingdom on other peoples and regions.

Had Simms not already reached his peak as a Southern American author with an international reputation, his work as the editor of a fledgling newspaper in the city of Columbia, South Carolina, might have been easily dismissed. It would have presented no threat to the reputation of a victorious Union army. The chances of his newspaper account going beyond the borders of the region would have been slim. What started as an attempt to discredit his reporting on the destruction of Columbia grew eventually into an attempt to discredit his work as a whole. Simms's idea of historians as balanced moral judges was not shared by Northern victors who were vulnerable to the claim that the very American ideals they were upholding had been violated. In time the story of the invasion of the South became dominated by historians intent on justifying the invasion. In such a scheme Simms's account served no acceptable purpose.[77]

But in the field of American literature, the situation was somewhat different. When the Nobel Prize–winner William Faulkner traveled to Japan in 1955, he prepared a nine-hundred-word message he titled "To the Youth of Japan." He commanded an international reputation that served to protect him when he opened his message with words that might well have been said by the forgotten William Gilmore Simms. Faulkner began with a summary of the War for Southern Independence: "My side, the South, lost that war, the battles of which were fought not on neutral ground in the waste of the ocean, but in our own homes, our gardens, our farms." Emphasizing the magnitude of the devastation, Faulkner continued: "Our land, our homes were invaded by a conqueror who remained after we were defeated; we were not only devastated by the battles . . . [but] the conqueror spent the next ten years after . . . despoiling us of what little war had left. The victors . . . made no effort to rehabilitate and reestablish us in any community of men or of nations."

Then Faulkner affirmed the power of the pen: "It is war and disaster which remind man most that he needs a record of his endurance and toughness. I think that is why . . . there rose in my country, the South, a resurgence of . . . writing . . . good enough . . . that people in other lands began to talk of a . . . Southern literature even until I, a countryman, have become one of the first names in our literature."[78]

Simms died in the midst of Radical Reconstruction and did not witness the continuing erosion of the South's political, economic, historical, and personal freedoms—a condition that Faulkner inherited at his birth. Dying only seven years after writing "To the Youth of Japan," Faulkner left his own record of the War for Southern Independence. He had, then, joined the thousands of American authors who had written on the bloodiest war of the nineteenth century, making it by far the most written about subject not only in American literature but also in the whole of American culture. But among all these thousands of authors and among all these tens of thousands of works, William Gilmore Simms's "The Capture, Sack, and Destruction of the City of Columbia" stands out both because it was written by the Father of Southern Literature and because it is a classic Jeffersonian critique of American consensual government gone awry. In Simms's war account the Northern invasion of the South is checked, not by any political or economic or cultural independence, but by the telling, writing, and remembering of the enormity of the burning of Columbia.

Notes

1. Edgar Lee Masters, *Lincoln: The Man* (New York: Dodd Mead, 1931), 399.

2. Ibid., 422–23.

3. William Gilmore Simms, "The Capture, Sack and Destruction of the City of Columbia," *Columbia Phoenix*, 28 March 1865.

4. James L. Vallandigham, *The Life of Clement L. Vallandigham* (Baltimore: Turnbull, 1872), 370.

5. Ibid., 333.

6. William P. Trent, *William Gilmore Simms* (Boston & New York: Houghton, Mifflin, 1892), 281.

7. Simms, "The Capture, Sack and Destruction of the City of Columbia," *Columbia Phoenix*, 21 March 1865.

8. Walter B. Edgar and Deborah K. Woolley, *Columbia: Portrait of a City* (Norfolk, Va.: Donning, 1986), 29.

9. J. Franklin Jameson, "Diary of Edward Hooker," *Annual Report of the American Historical Association* (Washington, D.C., 1897), I: 854; quoted in *Architecture of the Old South: South Carolina* by Mills Lane (New York: Abbeville Press, 1984), 101.

10. Edgar and Woolley, *Columbia: Portrait of a City*, 14.

11. Marion Brunson Lucas, *Sherman and the Burning of Columbia* (College Station & London: Texas A&M University Press, 1976), 20.

12. F. Y. Hedley, *Marching through Georgia* (Chicago: Donohue, Henneberry, 1890), 365–66.

13. Emma LeConte, *When the World Ended*, ed. Earl Schenck Miers (New York: Oxford University Press, 1957), 12.

14. Ibid., 62.

15. Lane, *Architecture of the Old South*, 158.

16. Ibid., 159.

17. Daniel Walker Hollis, *University of South Carolina* (Columbia: University of South Carolina Press, 1951), I:4, 135.

18. Lane, *Architecture of the Old South*, 186.

19. Ibid.

20. Blanche Marsh, *Robert Mills: Architect* (Columbia: R. L. Bryan, 1970), 98.

21. Ibid., 117.

22. Ibid., 95.

23. Ibid., 183.

24. Ibid., 86.

25. Charles Fraser, *Reminiscences of Charleston* (Charleston: John Russell, 1854).

26. Walter B. Edgar, *South Carolina: A History* (Columbia: University of South Carolina Press, 1998), 289.

27. Hollis, *University of South Carolina*, I:228.

28. Richard B. McCaslin, *Portrait of Conflict: A Photographic History of South Carolina in the Civil War* (Fayetteville: University of Arkansas Press, 1994), 42.

29. Ibid., 51.

30. James E. Kibler, "Simms the Gardener, Reconstructing the Gardens at Woodlands," *Simms Review* 1 (Summer 1993): 19.

31. Ibid., 28.

32. Juanita Kibler, *Dutch Fork Cookery: A Treasury of Traditional Recipes from the German Kitchens of Central South Carolina* (Athens, Ga.: Dutch Fork Press, 1989), 92.

33. Ibid., 91.

34. Alice G. B. Lockwood, ed., *Gardens of Colonies and of the Republic before 1840* (New York: Scribner's, 1934), 233–34.

35. *A Guide to Confederate Columbia* (Tuscaloosa, Ala.: Mary Noel Kershaw Foundation, 1996), 12.

36. Ibid., 43.

37. Hattie Kilgore and William P. McKinnon, eds., *Our Women of the War: A Series of Papers Written by Southern Ladies and Published in the South Carolina News and Courier* (Knoxville: Tennessee Valley Publishing, 1998), 180ff.

38. Ibid., 15.

39. *Pantheon and Repertoire of the Russian Stage* (November 1850), vol. 6, book 11, part 3:1; quoted in E. A. Morozkina and M. O. Erchtein, "W. G. Simms's Views and Works as Looked upon from Russia," *Simms Review* 9 (Summer 2001): 13.

40. Keen Butterworth, "William Gilmore Simms," in Dictionary of Literary Biography, vol. 3, *Antebellum Writers* in *New York and the South*, ed. Joel Myerson (Detroit: Gale Research, 1979), 313.

41. Mary C. Simms Oliphant, Alfred Taylor Odell, and T. C. Duncan Eaves, eds., *The Letters of William Gilmore Simms*, 6 vols. (Columbia: University of South Carolina Press, 1952–1956, 1983), IV: 178.

42. Ibid., V: 32.

43. Ibid., I: 123ff.

44. Ibid., III: 125.

45. Ibid., IV: 310.

46. Lewis P. Simpson, *The Dispossessed Garden: Pastoral and History in Southern Literature* (Athens: University of Georgia Press, 1975), 53.

47. *Letters*, I: 159ff.

48. James Everett Kibler, "William Gilmore Simms," in Dictionary of Literary Biography, volume 248: *Antebellum Writers in the South, Second Series*, ed. Kent Ljungquist (Detroit: Gale Group, 2002), 338.

49. Mrs. St. Julien Ravenel, *Charleston: The Place and the People* (New York: Macmillan, 1929), 304.

50. Kinloch Rivers, "Simms, the Man," *Simms Review* 2 (Winter 1994): 30.

51. Ibid, 29.

52. Simms, "Personal Memorabilia," Charles Carroll Simms Collection, South Caroliniana Library, University of South Carolina.

53. *Letters*, IV: 486.

54. LeConte, *When the World Ended*, 64–65.

55. Ibid., 80–81.

56. Ibid., 81.

57. Ibid., 82.

58. Ibid., 82.

59. *Columbia Phoenix*, 21 March 1865.

60. James Everett Kibler, "William Gilmore Simms," 290.

61. Ibid.

62. *Letters*, IV: 506, note 79.

63. George Ward Nichols, *The Story of the Great March* (New York: Harper, 1865), 277.

64. Ibid., 119. Sherman's letter to Fry is quoted in Mark Grimsley, *The Hard Hand of War* (New York: Cambridge University Press, 1995), 193.

65. Ibid., 118ff.

66. Ibid., 165.

67. William T. Sherman, *Memoirs* (New York: Appleton, 1875); republished, with an introduction, by William S. McFeely (New York: DaCapo, 1984), 286.

68. Nichols, *The Story of the Great March*, 166.

69. Ibid., 170–71.

70. Ibid., 149.

71. Hedley, *Marching through Georgia*, 361.

72. Ibid., 375.

73. Ibid., 388.

74. *Letters*, I: xxxii.

75. Ibid., I: xxxiv.

76. Simms, *Tales of the South*, ed. Mary Ann Wimsatt (Columbia: University of South Carolina Press, 1996), 3–4.

77. Two historians who have recognized some of the value of Simms's account are Charles Royster in his *The Destructive War* (New York: Knopf, 1991) and John G. Barrett in his *Sherman's March through the Carolinas* (Chapel Hill: University of North Carolina Press, 1956). Sean R. Busick's *A Sober Desire for History* (Columbia: University of South Carolina Press, 2005) calls attention to the significant contributions Simms made to American historiography as "one of the most popular, widely read historical writers of his day."

78. William Faulkner, *Essays, Speeches and Public Letters*, ed. James B. Meriwether. (New York: Random House, 1965), 82–83.

THE CAPTURE, SACK, AND DESTRUCTION OF THE CITY OF COLUMBIA

William Gilmore Simms

From the *Columbia Phoenix*
Published by Julian A. Selby
COLUMBIA, S.C., TUESDAY, 21 MARCH 1865, VOL. 1, NO. 1.

I.

It has pleased God, in that Providence which is so inscrutable to man, to visit our beautiful city with the most cruel fate which can ever befall States or cities.[1] He has permitted the cruel and malignant enemy[2] to penetrate our country almost without impediment; to pollute our homes with his presence; to rob and ravage our dwellings, and to commit three-fifths of our city to the flames. Eighty-four squares, out of one hundred and twenty-four (!) which the city contains, have been destroyed, with scarcely the exception of a single house. The ancient capitol building of the State—that venerable structure which, for seventy years, has echoed with the eloquence and wisdom of the most famous statesmen—is laid in ashes; six temples of the Most High God have shared the same fate; eleven banking establishments; the schools of learning, the shops of art and trade, of invention and manufacture; shrines equally of religion, benevolence, and industry; are all buried together in one congregated ruin. Humiliation spreads her ashes over our homes and garments, and the universal wreck exhibits only one common aspect of despair. It is for us, as succinctly but as fully as possible, and in the simplest language, to endeavor to make the melancholy record of our wretchedness, so that our sons may always remember, and the whole Christian world everywhere may read.

II.

When, by a crime, no less than blunder, Gen. Johnston[3] was removed from the command of our armies in Georgia, which he had conducted with such signal ability, there were not a few of our citizens who felt the impending danger, and trembled at the disastrous consequences which they partly foresaw. The removal of a General so fully in the confidence of his troops, who had so long baffled the conquests, if he could not arrest the march, of the enemy, was of itself a proceeding to startle the thoughtful mind. The enemy loudly declared his satisfaction at the event, and on repeated occasions since has expressed himself to the same effect. He was emboldened by the change, and almost instantly after, his successes became rapid and of the most decided character.

Gen. Johnston was by nature, no less than training and education, the very best of our generals to be opposed to Gen. Sherman. To the nervo sanguine temperament, eager and impetuous, of the latter, he opposed a moral and physical nature—calm, sedate, circumspect; cool, vigilant and wary—always patient and watchful of his moment—never rash or precipitate, but ever firm and decisive—his resources all regulated by a self-possessed will, and a mind in full possession of that military *coup d' oeil* which, grasping the remotest relations of the field, is, probably, the very first essential to a general having the control of a large and various army.

The error which took Hood[4] into the colder regions of Tennessee, at the beginning of winter, was one which the Yankee General was slow to imitate, especially as, in so moving, Hood necessarily left all the doors wide open which conducted to the seaboard. It required no effort of genius—nay, did not need even the suggestions of ordinary talent—to prompt the former to take the pathways which were thus laid open to him. Even had he not already conceived the propriety of forcing his way to the Atlantic coast, and to a junction with his shipping, the policy of then doing so would have been forced upon him by the proceeding of his rival, and by the patent fact that there were no impediments to such a progress. We had neither army nor general ready to impede his march. It suggested itself. The facility of such a progress was clear enough, and, with that quickness of decision which distinguishes the temperament of Sherman, he at once rushed into the open pathway.

The hasty levies of regular troops, collected by Hardee,[5] and the clans of scattered militia, gathered with great difficulty and untrained to service, were rather calculated to provoke his enterprise than to impede his march; and, laying waste as he went, after a series of small and unimportant skirmishes, he made his way to the coast, made himself master of Savannah, and, from the banks of that river, beheld, opened before him, all the avenues into and through South Carolina. It is understood that Hardee had in hand, to oppose this progress, something less than 10,000 men, while the force of Sherman was, in round numbers, something like 50,000, of which 38,000[6] consisted of infantry—the rest of artillery and cavalry.

III.

The destruction of Atlanta, the pillaging and burning of other towns of Georgia, and the subsequent devastation along the march of the enemy through Georgia, gave sufficient earnest of the treatment to be anticipated by South Carolina, should the same commander be permitted to make a like progress in our State. The Northern press furnished him with the *cri de guerre* to be sounded when he should cross our borders. *"Voe victis!"*—wo to the conquered!—woes unmitigated, unqualified, remorseless—in the case of a people which had been the first to sound the bugles of resistance to the encroachments of the Northern tyranny and usurpation! The howl of delight (such was the language of the Northern press) sent up by Sherman's legions, when they looked across the Savannah to the shores of Carolina, was the sure forerunner of the terrible fate which threatened our people, should the demonic furies be once let loose upon our lands. Our people felt all the danger. They felt that it required the first abilities, the most strenuous exertions, the most prompt and efficient reinforcements, to prevent the threatening catastrophe.

South Carolina had, for a long season, been made a sort of nursery for sick generals, and a sort of pasture ground for incompetence and imbecility. Hardee, though of acknowledged ability, and considered able as the leader of a corps, was not the man to grasp the business of a large army. All eyes looked to Gen. Johnston as the one man, next to Lee, to whom the duty should be confided and the trust. It was confidently hoped and believed that he would be restored to the command, and that adequate reinforcements would be furnished, to enable him, not only to meet the enemy, but to take the initiate in beating him from the ground which he had won. At all events, no one doubted that, with adequate supplies of men and materiel, Johnston would most effectually arrest the farther progress of the invaders.

Applications of the most urgent entreaty were addressed by our delegates and leading men in Congress to the President, urging these objects. But, with that dogged and obstinate will which our President seems to regard as a virtue, he declined to restore the commander whom he had already so greatly wronged, and, in respect to reinforcements, these were too tardily furnished, and in too small number to avail much in offering the requisite resistance to the foe. The reinforcements did not make their appearance in due season for a concentration of our strength at any one point, and our opposition to Sherman, everywhere, consisted of little more than a series of small skirmishes, without result on either side. No pass was held with any tenacity; no battle fought; the enemy were allowed to travel one hundred and fifty miles of our State, through a region of swamp and thicket, in no portion of which could a field be found adequate to the display of ten thousand men, and where, under good partisan leaders, the invaders might have been cut off in separate bodies, their supplies stopped, their march constantly embarrassed by hard fighting, and where, a bloody toll exacted at every defile, they must have found a Thermopylae[7] at every five miles of their march. We had no partisan fighting, as in the days of old.[8] We had a system which insisted upon artillery as paramount—insisted upon arbitrary lines for defence, chosen without any regard to the topography of the country. "We will make a stand," said our chiefs, "at this river crossing or that; then fall back to the next river, and so on to the last." Although, in a thousand places of dense swamp, narrow defile, and almost impenetrable thicket, between these rivers, it would have been easy to find spots where three hundred men, under competent commanders, who knew the country, might most effectually have baffled three thousand. At this very moment, while we write, we doubt if the scattered members of our army have yet been able to rendezvous together for the arrest of Sherman's progress to the coast or through North Carolina. But to return.[9]

IV.

The march of the enemy into our State was characterized by such scenes of brutality, license, plunder and general conflagration, as very soon showed that the threat of the Northern press, and of their soldiery, were not to be regarded as mere *brutum fulmen*.[10] Day by day, brought to the people of Columbia tidings of newer atrocities committed, and a wider and more extended progress. Daily did long trains of fugitives line the roads, with wives and children, and horses and stock and cattle, seeking refuge from the wolfish fury which pursued. Long lines of wagons covered the highways. Half naked people cowered from the winter under bush tents in the thickets, under the eaves of houses, under the railroad sheds, and in old cars left them along the route. All these repeated the same story of brutal outrage and great suffering, violence, poverty and nakedness. Habitation after habitation, village after village—one sending up its signal flames to the other, presaging for it the same fate—lighted the winter and midnight sky with crimson horrors. All houses which had been left vacant were first robbed and then destroyed; and where the families still ventured to remain, they were, in most instances, so tortured by insult, violence, robbery and all manner of brutality, that flight became necessary, and the burning of the dwelling soon followed the flight of the owner. No language can describe the sufferings of these fugitives, or the demonic horrors by which they were pursued; nor can any catalogue furnish an adequate detail of the wide-spread destruction of homes and property. Granaries were emptied, and where the grain was not carried off, it was strewn to waste under the feet of their cavalry or consigned to the fire which consumed the dwelling. The negroes were robbed equally with the whites of food and clothing. The roads were covered with butchered cattle, hogs, mules and the costliest furniture. Nothing was permitted to escape. Valuable cabinets, rich pianos, were not only hewn to pieces, but bottles of ink, turpentine, oil, whatever could efface or destroy, upon which they could conveniently lay hands, was employed to defile and ruin. Horses were ridden into the houses. Sick people were forced from their beds, to permit the search after hidden treasures. In pursuit of these, the most diabolic ingenuity was exercised, and the cunning of the Yankee, in robbing, proved far superior to that of the negro for concealment. The beautiful homesteads of the parish country, with their wonderful tropical gardens, were ruined; ancient dwellings of black cypress, one hundred years old, which had been reared by the fathers of the republic—men whose names were famous in Revolutionary history—were given to the torch as recklessly as were the rudest hovels; the ancient furniture was hewn to pieces; the costly collections of China were crushed wantonly under foot; choice pictures and works of art, from Europe; select and numerous libraries, objects of peace wholly; were all destroyed. The summer retreats, simple cottages of slight and unpretending structure, were equally devoted to the flames, and, where the dwellings were not destroyed—and they were only spared while the inhabitants resolutely remained in them—they were robbed of all their portable contents, and what the plunderer could not bear away, was ruthlessly hewn to pieces. The inhabitants, black no less than white, were left to starve, compelled to feed only upon the garbage to be found in the abandoned camps of the enemy. The corn scraped up from the spots where the horses fed, has been the only means of life left to thousands but lately in affluence. It was the avowed policy of the enemy to reach our armies through the sufferings of their women and children—to starve out the families of those gallant soldiers whom they had failed to subdue in battle.

And thus plundering, destroying, burning, they made their way through a portion of Beaufort into Barnwell District, where they pursued the same game. The villages of Buford's Bridge, of Barnwell, Blackville, Graham's, Bamberg, Midway, were more or less destroyed; the wretched inhabitants everywhere left homeless and without food. The horses and mules, all cattle and hogs, whenever fit for service or for food, were stolen, and all the rest shot. Every implement of the workman or the farmer, tools, plows, hoes, gins, looms, wagons, vehicles, was made to feed the flames.

From Barnwell to Orangeburg and Lexington was the next progress, marked everywhere by the same sweeping destruction. Both of these court towns were burned—the former partially, the latter wholly. Both were thoroughly plundered of all valuables which could be carried away.

V.

Tidings of these atrocities duly reached the people of Columbia, and might have prepared them for the treatment they were destined to receive. Daily accessions of fugitives flying before the enemy, bringing with them their valuables and provisions, made ample report of the horrid progress of the ruffianly despoiler. Hundreds of families had seasonably left long before, in anticipation of the danger. Columbia was naturally held to be one of the most secure places of refuge. It was never doubted that this capital city, which contained so many of the manufactures of the Confederate Government, the treasury, &c., would be defended with all the concentrated vigor of which the Confederacy was capable, especially, too, as upon the several railroads connected with the city, the army of Lee and the safety of Richmond were absolutely dependent. Young women of family were sent in large numbers to a city, where numbers seemed to promise a degree of security not to be hoped for in any obscure rural abode. The city was accordingly doubled in population, and here also was to be found an accumulation of wealth, in plate, jewels, pictures, books, manufactures of art and *virtu*, not to be estimated—not, perhaps, to be paralleled in any other town of the Confederacy. In many instances, the accumulations were those of a hundred years—of successive generations—in the hands of the oldest families of the South. A large proportion of the wealth of Charleston had been stored in the capital city, and the owners of these treasures, in many instances, were unable to effect any farther remove. If apprehensive of the danger, they could only fold their hands and, hoping against hope, pray for escape from a peril to which they could oppose no farther vigilance or effort.

Still, the lurking belief with most persons, who apprehended the approach of the enemy, encouraged the faith that, as the city was wholly defenceless—as no attempt would be made to defend it—in the event of a summons, it would be surrendered upon the usual terms, and that these would necessarily insure the safety of non-combatants and protect their property.

But, in truth, there was no small portion of the inhabitants who denied or doubted, almost to the last moment, that the enemy contemplated any serious demonstration upon the city. They assumed—and this idea was tacitly encouraged, if not believed, by the authorities, military and civil—that the movement on Columbia was but a feint, and that the bulk of Sherman's army was preparing for a descent upon Charleston. This also seemed to be the opinion in Charleston itself. It was understood, or so reported, in Columbia, that the force pressing upon our troops in this direction consisted of but 6,000 men, while, to oppose them, we had 7,000.

VI.

All these conjectures were speedily set at rest, when, on the 13th February, (Monday,) the enemy was reported to have reached a point in Lexington District, some ten miles above Jeffcoat's. On the 14th, their progress brought them to Thom's Creek, the stream next below Congaree Creek, and about twelve miles below the city. Here our troops, consisting of the mounted gunmen of Hampton, Wheeler, Butler, &c.,[11] made stubborn head against them, holding them in check by constant skirmishing. This skirmishing continued throughout Wednesday, but failed to arrest the enemy's progress; and as their cannon continued momently to sound more heavily upon our ears, we were but too certainly assured of the hopelessness of the struggle. The odds of force against us were too vast for any valor or generalship to make head against it; and yet, almost to this moment, the hope was held out to the people, in many quarters, that the city could be saved. It was asserted that the corps of Cheatham and Stewart[12] were making forced marches, with the view to a junction with the troops under Beauregard, and, such was the spirit of our troops, and one of the generals at least, that almost at the moment when Sherman's advance was entering the town, Hampton's cavalry was in order of battle, and only waiting the command to charge it. But the horrors of a street fight in a defenceless city, filled with women and children, were prudently avoided; and our gallant troops were drawn off from the scene at the very hour when the enemy were entering upon it. But we anticipate.

VII.

Whatever hopes might have been entertained of the ultimate success of our defences, they were all dissipated, when, by daylight, on the 16th, (Thursday,) our troops re-entered the city, burning the several bridges over the Congaree, the Broad and Saluda Rivers. They were quartered through the day about the several streets, and along their several bivouacs they dug slight excavations in the earth, as for rifle pits and for protection from the enemy's shells, which fell fast and thick about the town. They had commenced shelling the evening before, and continued it throughout the night. No summons for surrender had been made; no warning of any kind was given. The shelling continued throughout the day, and new batteries were in rapid progress of erection on the West side of the Congaree, the more effectually to press the work of destruction. The damage was comparatively slight. The new capitol building was struck five times, but suffered little or no injury. Numerous shells fell into the inhabited portions of the town, yet we hear of only two persons killed—one on the hospital square, and another near the South Carolina Railroad Depot. The venerable Mr. S. J. Wagner, from Charleston, an aged citizen of near eighty, narrowly escaped with life, a shell bursting at his feet. His face was excoriated by the fragments, and for awhile his eye-sight was lost; but we are happy to state that the hurts were slight, and he is now as well as ever.

On Wednesday, the 15th, the city was placed under martial law and the authority confided to Gen. E. M. Law.[13] With characteristic energy, this officer executed his trusts, and was employed day and night in the maintenance of order. This, with some few exceptions, was surprisingly maintained. It was indeed wonderful that, with so many soldiers in town, with so much confusion among the people, there should have been so little disorder. There was some riotous conduct after night. Some highway robberies were committed, and some few stores broken open and robbed. But, beyond these instances, there were but few instances of crime, and none of insubordination. Terrible, meanwhile, was the press, the shock, the rush, the hurry, the universal confusion—such as might naturally be looked for, in the circumstances of the city from which thousands were preparing to fly, without previous preparations for flight—burdened with pale and trembling women, their children and portable chattels—trunks and jewels, family Bibles and the *lares familiares*. The railroad depot for Charlotte was crowded with anxious waiters upon the train—with a wilderness of luggage —millions, perhaps, in value—much of which was left finally and lost. Throughout Tuesday, Wednesday and Thursday, these scenes of struggle were in constant performance. The citizens fared badly. The Governments of the State and of the Confederacy absorbed all the modes of conveyance. Transportation about the city could not be had, save by a rich or favored few. No love could persuade where money failed to convince and SELF, growing bloated in its dimensions, stared one from every hurrying aspect, as you traversed the excited and crowded streets. In numerous instances, those who succeeded in getting away did so at the cost of trunks and luggage and, under what discomforts they departed, no one who did not see can readily conceive.

VIII.

The end was rapidly approaching. The enemy's thunders were resounding at the gates. Defence was impossible. At a late hour on Thursday night, the Governor,[14] with his suite and a large train of officials, departed. The army began its evacuation, and by daylight few remained who were not resigned to the necessity of seeing the tragedy played out. After all the depletion, the city contained, according to our estimate, at least 20,000 inhabitants, the larger proportion being females and children and negroes. Hampton's cavalry, as we have already mentioned, lingered till near 10 o'clock the next day, and scattered groups of Wheeler's command hovered about the enemy at their entrance into the town.

The inhabitants were startled at daylight, on Friday morning, by a heavy explosion. This was the South Carolina Railroad Depot. It was accidentally blown up. Broken open by a band of plunderers, mostly low persons, among whom were many females and negroes, their reckless greed precipitated their fate. This building had been made the receptacle of supplies from sundry quarters, and was crowded with stores of merchants and planters, trunks of treasure, innumerable wares and goods of fugitives—all of great value. It appears that, among its contents, were some kegs of powder. The robbers paid, and suddenly, the penalties of their crime. Using their lights freely and hurriedly, the better to *pick*, as they stole, they fired a train of powder leading to the kegs. The explosion followed, and the number of persons destroyed is variously estimated, from seventeen to fifty. It is probable that not more than thirty-five suffered, but the actual number perishing is, to this moment, unascertained.

At an early hour on Friday, the commissary and quartermaster stores were thrown wide, the contents cast out into the streets and given to the people. The negroes especially loaded themselves with plunder. All this might have been saved, had the officers been duly warned by the military authorities of the probable issue of the struggle. Wheeler's cavalry also shared largely of this plunder, and several of them might be seen, even to the hour of the enemy's arrival, bearing off huge bales upon their saddles.

It was proposed that the white flag should be displayed from the tower of the City Hall. But Gen. Hampton, whose command had not yet left the city, and who was still eager to do battle in its defence, indignantly declared that if displayed, he should have it torn down. Up to this moment, his resolve was to fight the enemy in the streets, and, anxious to the last to try the effect of a charge upon the enemy's advance, he slowly retired from the city.

The following letter from the Mayor to Gen. Sherman was the initiation of the surrender:

MAYOR'S OFFICE,
Columbia, S.C., February 17, 1865.

To MAJOR-GENERAL SHERMAN: The Confederate forces having evacuated Columbia, I deem it my duty, as Mayor and representative of the city, to ask for its citizens the treatment accorded by the usages of civilized warfare. I therefore respectfully request that you will send a sufficient guard in advance of the army to maintain order in the city and protect the persons and property of the citizens.

Very respectfully, your obedient servant,

T. J. GOODWYN, Mayor.

At 9 o'clock, on the painfully memorable morning of the 17th February, (Friday,) a deputation from the City Council, consisting of the Mayor, Aldermen McKenzie, Bates and Stork,[15] in a carriage bearing a white flag, proceeded towards the Broad River Bridge Road. Arriving at the forks of the Winnsboro Road, they discovered that our skirmishers were still busy with their guns, playing upon the advance of the enemy. These were troops of General Wheeler. This conflict was continued simply to afford the main army all possible advantages of a start in their retreat. Gen. W. apprised the deputation that his men would now be withdrawn, and instructed them in what manner to proceed. The deputation met the column of the enemy under Capt. Platt,[16] who sent them forward to Col. Stone, who finally took his seat with them in the carriage. The advance belonged to the 15th corps, (Gen. Howard)[17] and this corps, we are told, is the one usually sent in advance when the purpose is destruction. It is tacitly understood in the army that the occupation of a city by the 15th corps is virtually its doom. It is very certain that these troops had long before become experts in the business of a sack, thorough pillage and all manner of incendiarism.

The Mayor reports that on surrendering the city to Col. Stone,[18] the latter assured him of the safety of the citizens and of the protection of their property *while under his command.* He could not answer for Gen. Sherman, who was in the rear, but he expressed the conviction that he would fully confirm the assurances which he (Col. Stone) had given, Subsequently, Gen. Sherman did confirm them, and that night, seeing that the Mayor was exhausted by his labors of the day, he counselled him to retire to rest, saying, "Not a finger's breadth, Mr. Mayor, of your city shall be harmed. You may lie down to sleep, satisfied that your town shall be as safe in my hands as if wholly in your own." Such was very nearly the language in which he spoke; such was the substance of it. He added: "It will become my duty to destroy some of the public or Government buildings; but I will reserve this performance to another day. It shall be done tomorrow, provided the day be calm." And the Mayor retired with this solemnly asserted and repeated assurance.

[CONTINUED IN OUR NEXT.]

The Fire.

The following is a list of the owners and occupants of the houses destroyed:[19]

RICHARDSON OR MAIN STREET.
Cotton Town.—West Side.

Wm Price. Warehouse filled with cotton.

W McAlister and R Keenan, jr. Dwelling.

James Cathcart. Store and warehouse filled with cotton.

R O'Neale. 2 warehouses filled with cotton.

P P Chambers. Warehouse filled with cotton.

Mrs J J Kinsler. Dwelling.

Mrs Law. Store and warehouse containing provisions belonging to
    Dr A W Kennedy.

East.

James Crawford. Dwelling.

R. O'Neale. Store and warehouse containing a quantity of cotton.

J R Kennedy. Dwelling.

L D Childs. Dwelling and out houses.

The houses of A Civil and Jas Tarrar saved.

Upper to Lumber.—West.

Mrs Kirk. Store, dwelling, etc, occupied by Mrs Cartwright.

Estate Jas A Kennedy. Storehouse containing Government provisions.

Estate Jas A Kennedy. Dwelling occupied by A Boney, M P Brennan and others.

P H Flanigan. Store and dwelling occupied by Milroy.

G B Nunamaker. Store, dwelling, cotton house, etc.

A Crawford. Cotton warehouse.

"   "   Dwelling occupied by Mrs J Jacobs and C Agnew.

East.

Kraft, Goldsmith & Kraft. Sword factory.

Henry Hunt. Dwelling.

Mrs P Patterson. Dwelling occupied by Dr I D Durham.

St Mary's College. Government stores, etc.

R Lewis. Store and dwelling occupied by R Caldwell and Government goods.

Wm Lyles. Store and dwelling.

Lumber to Richland.—West.

Wm Hennies. Store and warehouse used as cooper's shop and Government storehouse

Wm Hennies. Dwelling occupied by owner, store filled with Government goods

H Hess. Store and dwelling

"   Store filled with furniture

Grieshabers & Wolfe. 2 stores and dwelling

Dr T J Roach. Dwelling oc by Molleuhauer

M McElrone. Dwelling

East.

John Judge & Co. Stocking factory

A Riley. Store and dwelling

"   Dwelling occupied by

W McGuinnis. Store and dwelling.

A Riley. Store and dwelling occupied by P Pinkersson

The dwelling owned by A Riley and occupied by Mr Huchet was not burnt.[20]

Richland to Laurel.—West.

Estate John Beard. Dwelling occupied by S Mathews, store used by State Commissary

Mrs J Blankenstein. Store and dwelling occupied by John Mason

Mrs J Blankenstein. Store and dwelling occupied by M Thomer and others

M O'Connell. Store and dwelling

A J Barnes. Store and dwelling occupied by M Thompson

W W Purse. Store and dwelling

R Lewis. Store occupied by J Fraser & Co.

    "   Vacant store

    "   Store used for Government stores

East.

Bishop Lynch. Dwellings occupied by Ponsignon and others

John McCully. Dwelling, store occupied by F D Fanning

H C Franck. Dwelling

Mrs Law. Dwelling, store used as Government warehouse

Laurel to Blanding.—West.

Keatinge & Ball. Engraving establishment

Estate C Beck. Dwelling occupied by John Davis and others

Dr F Marks. Store occupied by   , dwellings by
    F Marks, J A Patton and others

Estate John J Kinsler. Dwelling occupied by Jos Sampson and others, store by
    A Jones

Estate John Kinsler. Store oc by H Reckling

David Jacobs. Dwelling

M Comerford. Store and dwelling occupied by H Kaufman

M Comerford. Store and dwelling

East.

Boyne & Sprowl. Stone Yard

Estate C Beck. Store occupied by J C Kenneth, dwelling by N Thompson
    and others

Jamos [sic; James] Brown. Government stores

Thos Boyne. Dwelling

C Norman. Store occupied by Mrs Hertwig

    "   "   "   "   J. Mendel

    "   Dwelling   "   "

E Stenhouse. Store and dwelling

E Hope. Store occupied by H Hunt, dwelling by W Phelps

E Hope. Store occupied by A Miles

E & G D Hope. Store, sleeping rooms occupied by P Schwartz, A Koepper
    and others

Blanding to Taylor or Camden.—West.

R Bryce. Store occupied by M S [Mutual Supply] Associat'n
"   "   "   Mrs DuRoss
"   Dwelling occupied by Mrs D C Speck as a boarding house
M Ehrlich. Shoe store and dwelling
"   Store occupied by W Stieglitz
John Seegers. Store occupied by J Bahlman
"   "   "   Miss K Frank
Bruns & Eilhardt. Shoe store and dwelling
John Rawls. Store occupied by John S Due
"   Barber's shop oc by C Carroll
"   Store occupied by
"   "   "   P Pape
W T Walter. Store occupied by Mrs. Zernow, dwelling by
W T Walter. Express Co, unclaimed freight
"   Dwelling unoccupied
"   Store occupied by L Blum
Estate J J Kinsler. Store occupied by L C Clarke
"   "   Store occupied by Sill & Sill
"   Rooms in second story used by Evans & Cogswell as
lithographic office, third story as Treasury Note Bureau

East.

Bishop Lynch. Ursuline Convent and Acad
"   Store occupied by A Traeger
"   "   "   J Blank
S Pearse. Residence
"   Store occupied by F A Jacobs
"   "   "   P G McGregor
H N McGowan. Store occupied by V Heidt
"   "   "   Miss Evans
"   Dwelling occ'd by W K Sessford
Fisher & Heinitsh. Store
"   Dwelling occ'd by E Egg
S Gardner. Store and residence
"   Store occupied by .
S Pearse. Store; dwelling oc by J Barry
"   House occup'd by colored families
H Henrichson. Store

S Gardner. Store occupied by J J Browne and W Ashton
S Gardner. Dwelling occup'd by J Burnside
"   Exchange Bank

Blanding [Taylor] to Plain—West.

Commercial Bank, dwelling occ'd by H Scott
"   Store oc by Farmer's & Ex'e [Exchange] Bk
Thomas Davis. M H Berry and J J Cohen, dwelling by Adams
Thomas Davis. Dwelling oc by A Reckling
H Davis. Store occupied by Silcox, Bro & Co, dwelling by Geo Smith
H Davis. Store occ'd by Hopson & Sutphen, rooms above as War Tax Office
Henry Davis. Store oc by T & R Flanigan
"   "   J S Bird & Co, second floor as Zealy's daguerrean rooms
Henry Davis. Store occupied by Mad [Madame] A Fillette, residence by
   Dr. Solomons
Henry Davis. Store occupied by R Swaffield and P Wineman & Co
Henry Davis. Bank of Charleston
R C Anderson. Store occ'ed by D Goldstein
"   Store
"   S W R R Bank [Southwestern Railroad Bank]
"   Transportation office, second story as Government offices

East.

Southern Express Co's office, second and third floors occupied by Mad
   [Madame] Rutjes as boarding house
So Ex Co. [Southern Express Company] Store occupied by John Veal
Estate C Beck. Store oc'd by Mrs D Jacobs
"   Residence and store occupied by Mrs M S Cooper, Miss M L
Poindexter, J W Gaither and family and others
Isaac Cohen. Store occupied by T J Moise and F C Jacobs
Isaac Cohen. Store and residence occupied by John McKenzie
G V Antwerp. Store occupied by W M & J C Martin, People's Bank and
   Reynolds & Reynolds, residence by Dr Wm L Reynolds
G V Antwerp. Store occupied by Dr P M Cohen, G Diercks and Geo Bruns
Chas Black. Store occupied by W S Harral and J Marsh, residence by J
   Chrietzberg
Dr M M Sams. Store occupied by J B Duval & Son, residence by Wm Watson
Dr M M Sams. Store occupied by J F Eisenman & Co, residence by G V
   Antwerp
Thos Davis. Store occupied by John Heise, 2d and 3d floors by J N Roach and
   J Richard

Thos Davis. Store by Mrs S A Smith, rooms by I C Morgan
Thos Davis. Store occupied by R Henning, residence by Misses Saunders
Dr C Wells. Store occupied by Townsend & North, residence by J B Duval
     and W Lalloo
Dr C Wells. Union Bank

[CONTINUED IN OUR NEXT.]

COLUMBIA, S.C., THURSDAY, 23 MARCH 1865, VOL. 1, NO. 2.

IX.

At about 11 o'clock, the head of the column, following the deputation—the flag of the United States surmounting the carriage—reached Market Hall, on Main street, while that of the corps was carried in the rear. On their way to the city, the advance was fired upon by some scattered troopers of Wheeler's command, and Col. Stone said to the Mayor, "We shall hold you responsible for this outrage." We are particular in mentioning this fact, as we believe that subsequently, the incident has been urged by some of the enemy as a justification of the sack and burning of the city. The Mayor made a suitable apology, and pointed to the fact which was obvious enough, that the act was that of some unauthorized stragglers, lingering in the rear of our army.

Hardly had the troops reached the head of Main street, when the work of pillage was begun. Stores were broken open in the presence of thousands within the first hour after their arrival. The contents, when too cumbersome for the plunderers, were cast into the streets. Gold and silver, jewels and liquors, were eagerly sought. No attempt was made to arrest the burglars. The authorities, officers, soldiers, all, seemed to consider it a matter of course. And wo to him who carried a watch with gold chain pendant; or who wore a choice hat, or overcoat, or boots or shoes. He was stripped by ready experts in the twinkling of an eye. It is computed that, from first to last, twelve hundred watches were transferred from the pockets of their owners to those of the robbers. Purses shared the same fate; nor was Confederate currency repudiated. But of all these things hereafter, in more detail.

At about 12 o'clock, the jail was discovered to be on fire from within. This building was immediately in the rear of the Market, or City Hall, and in a densely built portion of the city. It had held a large body of prisoners, who had been seasonably removed several days before, along with others at the Asylum—some 1,500 of them having been gotten off from the city successfully, by extraordinary exertions on the part of Capt. Sharpe,[21] the chief of transportation. The fire of the jail had been preceded by that of some cotton piled in the streets. Both fires were soon subdued by the firemen. At about 1 1/2 P.M., that of the jail was rekindled, and was again extinguished. Some of the prisoners, by-the-way, had made their escape, in some instances, a few days before, and were secreted and protected by citizens. A person named Morris, charged with a most deliberate and cruel murder of a man named Hicks, was one of those who escaped at the last moment; and he, it is said, showed himself active in pointing out to the enemy, as proper objects of odium, all persons to whom he himself was hostile, including others who were held to be proper objects of punishment or plunder.

The experience of the firemen in putting out the fires in the cotton and jail building were of a sort to discourage their farther efforts. They were thwarted and embarrassed by the continued interference of the soldiery. Finally, their hose was chopped with swords and axes, or pierced with bayonets, so as to be rendered useless. The engines were in some cases demolished also. And so the miserable day wore on, in pillage, insult, and constant confusion and alarm. No one could persuade himself to feel the security which had been promised to person and property. No one felt safe in his own dwelling; and in the faith that, as Gen. Sherman was a Catholic,[22] and would, no doubt, spare the convent of his church, especially as the Mother Superior had, years before, been the teacher of his own children, numbers of young ladies were confided to the care of that lady, and even trunks of clothes and treasure were sent thither, in full confidence that they would find safety. Vain illusions! *The Irish Catholic troops, it appears, were not brought into the city at all; were kept on the other side of the river, and were thus relieved from the odium of the crimes which followed, as well as denied the privilege of succoring the people of their own faith.* But a few Catholics were collected among the corps which occupied the city, and of the conduct of these, a favorable account is given. One of them rescued a silver goblet of the church, used as a drinking cup by a soldier, and restored it to the Rev. Dr. O'Connell. This priest, by the way, was knocked down and severely handled by the soldiers. Such, also, was the fortune of the Rev. Mr. Shand,[23] of Trinity (the Episcopal) Church, who sought in vain to save a trunk containing the sacred vessels of his church. It was violently wrested from his keeping, and his struggle to save it only provoked the rougher usage. We are since told that, on reaching Camden, General Sherman restored these vessels to Bishop Davis; an act which betrayed his thorough acquaintance with the general robbery and his sanction of it. This sack and firing seem equally reduced to system.

X.

And here it may be well to mention, as suggestive of many clues, an incident which presented a sad commentary on that confidence in the security of the convent, which was entertained by the great portion of the people. This establishment, under the charge of the sister of the Right Rev. Bishop Lynch, was at once a convent and an academy of the highest class. Hither were sent for education the daughters of Protestants, of the most wealthy classes throughout the State; and these, with the nuns and those young ladies sent thither on the emergency, probably exceeded one hundred. The Lady Superior herself entertained the fullest confidence in the immunities of the establishment. But her confidence was clouded, after she had enjoyed a conference with a certain major of the Yankee army, who described himself as an editor from Detroit. He visited her at an early hour in the day, and announced his friendly sympathies with the Lady Superior and the sisterhood; professed his anxiety for their safety—his purpose to do all that he could to insure it—declared that he would instantly go to Sherman and secure a chosen guard, and, altogether, made such professions of love and service as to disarm those suspicions, which bad looks and bad manners, inflated speech and pompous carriage, might otherwise have provoked. The Lady Superior, with such a charge in her hands, was naturally glad to welcome all shows and prospects of support, and expressed her gratitude. He disappeared, and soon after re-appeared, bringing with him no less than eight or ten men— none of them, as he admitted, being Catholics. He had some specious argument to show that, perhaps, her guard had better be one of Protestants. This suggestion staggered the lady a little, but he seemed to convey a more potent reason, when he added, in a whisper: *"For I must tell you, my sister, that Columbia is a doomed city!"* Terrible doom! This creature, leaving his tools behind him, disappeared to show himself no more. The guards so left behind were finally among the most busy as plunderers. The moment that the inmates, driven out by the fire, were forced to abandon their house, they began to revel in its contents. *Quis custodiet ipsos custodes?*—who shall guard the guards?—asks the proverb. In half the number of cases, the guards provided for the citizens were among the most active plunderers, were quick to betray their trusts, abandon their posts, and bring their comrades in to join in the general pillage. The most dextrous and adroit of these, it is the opinion of most persons, were chiefly Eastern men, or men of immediate Eastern origin—probably the experts through a long course of training, of the larger cities, graduating finally at Sing-Sing and other places of mental and moral training. The Western men, including the Indiana, and a portion of the Illinois and Iowa, were neither so dextrous nor so unscrupulous— were frequently faithful and respectful; and, perhaps, it would be safe to assert that many of the houses which escaped the sack and fire, owed their safety to the presence or the contiguity of some of these men. Ruder of speech and manner than the Eastern men, rough and surly perhaps, they lacked equally the impudence, pretension, pomposity and utter indifference to truth, honesty and shame, which distinguished the latter. But we must retrace our steps.

William Gilmore
Simms, circa 1865.
Courtesy of the South
Caroliniana Library,
University of South
Carolina, Columbia,
S.C.

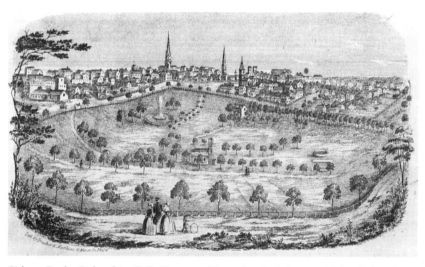

Sidney Park, Columbia, S.C. Engraved letterhead, 6 August 1854, Colin C.
Murchison Papers, South Caroliniana Library. Courtesy of the South Caroliniana Library.

Hugo Bosse, "Sketch in the Center of the City of Columbia, S.C." *New York Illustrated News*, 1861. Courtesy of the South Caroliniana Library.

"Wade Hampton's Garden, Columbia, South Carolina." *Harper's Weekly Magazine*, 8 April 1865. Courtesy of the South Caroliniana Library.

"View of Wade Hampton's Residence, Columbia, South Carolina." *Harper's Weekly Magazine*, 15 April 1865. Courtesy of the South Caroliniana Library.

"General Sherman's Entry into Columbia, South Carolina, February 17, 1865." *Harper's Weekly Magazine*, 1 April 1865. Courtesy of the South Caroliniana Library.

J. E. Taylor, "The 13th Iowa Regiment, of the 17th Corps, Raising the Stars and Stripes upon the State House at Columbia, S.C." *Frank Leslie's Illustrated Magazine*, 8 April 1865. Courtesy of the South Caroliniana Library.

William Waud, "The Burning of Columbia, South Carolina, February 17, 1865." *Harper's Weekly Magazine*, 8 April 1865. Courtesy of the South Caroliniana Library.

Columbia Jail, 1865. Photograph by Richard Wearn. Courtesy of the South Caroliniana Library.

Presbyterian Lecture Room, 1865. Photograph by Richard Wearn. Courtesy of the South Caroliniana Library.

View of Main Street from the State House, 1865. Photograph by Richard
Wearn. Courtesy of the South Caroliniana Library.

Main Street, Columbia, 1865. The uncompleted State House is on the right.
Photograph by Richard Wearn. Courtesy of the South Caroliniana Library.

Theodore R. Davis, "Among the Ruins of Columbia, South Carolina." *Harper's Weekly Magazine*, 21 July 1865. Courtesy of the South Caroliniana Library.

Theodore R. Davis, "The Ruins of Columbia, South Carolina—Richardson Street, Looking toward the Capitol." *Harper's Weekly Magazine*, 21 July 1865. Courtesy of the South Caroliniana Library.

SACK AND DESTRUCTION

of the

CITY OF COLUMBIA. S. C.

to which is added

A LIST OF THE PROPERTY DESTROYED.

COLUMBIA, S. C.:
POWER PRESS OF DAILY PHŒNIX,
1865.

Title page for the 1865 pamphlet version of Simms's account. Courtesy of the South Caroliniana Library.

The *Columbia Phoenix*, 1 April 1865, which includes parts 20 through 25 of Simms's account of the destruction of Columbia. Courtesy of the South Caroliniana Library.

XI.

It may be well to remark that the discipline of the enemy upon their first entrance into the city was perfect and most admirable. There was no disorder or irregularity on the line of march, showing that their officers had them completely in hand. They were a fine looking body of men, mostly young and of vigorous formation, well clad and well shod, seemingly wanting in nothing. Their arms and accoutrements were in bright order. The negroes accompanying them were not numerous, and seemed mostly to act as drudges and body servants. They groomed horses, waited, carried burdens, and, in almost every instance under our eyes, appeared in a purely servile, and not a military, capacity. The men of the West treated them generally with scorn or indifference, sometimes harshly, and not unfrequently with blows. Most of those escaping from them since their departure—and they have been numerous—express themselves sufficiently satisfied with their brief taste of Yankee fraternity.

But, if the march of the enemy into town and while on duty, was indicative of admirable drill and discipline, such ceased to be the case the moment they were dismissed. Then, whether by tacit permission or direct command, their whole deportment underwent a sudden and rapid change. The demonic saturnalia soon began. We have shown that the robbery of the persons of the citizens and the plunder of their houses commenced within one hour after they had reached the Market Hall. It continued without interruption throughout the day. Sherman, at the head of his cavalry, traversed the streets everywhere—so did his officers— yet they saw nothing to rebuke or restrain. Subsequently, these officers were everywhere on foot, yet beheld nothing which required the interposition of authority. Robbery was going on at every corner—in every house—yet there was no censure, no punishment. Citizens generally applied for a guard at their several houses, and, for a time, these guards were allotted them. They consisted usually of two soldiers—a sergeant and a private. These might be faithful or not. In some cases, as already stated, they were, and civil and respectful; considerate of the claims of women, and never trespassing upon the privacy of the family; but, in half the number of cases, at least, they were intrusive, insulting and treacherous—leaving no privacy undisturbed, passing without a word into the chambers and prying into every crevice and corner. They were so many spies set upon the homestead, to become plunderers when the chance was afforded them; and, failing in opportunity to make it, by firing the dwelling, in concert with their comrades without, and, after expelling the inmates, through the terrors they inspired, proceeding to the work of pillage without embarrassment from any quarter.

But the reign of terror did not fairly begin till night. In some instances, where parties complained of the misrule and robbery, their guards said to them, with a chuckle: "This is nothing. Wait till to-night, and you'll see h-ll." Hell it was, and these wretches the demons all let loose!

Among the first fires at evening was one about dark, which broke out in a filthy purlieu of low houses, of wood, on Gervais street, occupied mostly as brothels. Almost at the same time, a body of the enemy scattered over the Eastern outskirts of the city, fired severally the dwellings of Mr. Secretary Trenholm, Gen. Wade Hampton, Dr. John Wallace, J. U. Adams, Mrs. Starke, Mr. Latta, Mrs. English and many others. There were then some twenty fires in full blast, in as many different quarters, at nearly the same moment; and while the alarm sounded from these quarters, a similar alarm was sent up almost simultaneously from Cotton Town, the Northermost limit of the city, and from Main street in its very centre, at the several stores or houses of O. B. Bates, C. D. Eberhardt and some others, in the heart of the most densely settled portion of the town; thus enveloping in flames almost every section of the devoted city. At this period, thus early in the evening, there were few shows of that drunkenness which prevailed at a late hour in the night, and only after all the grocery shops on Main street had been rifled. The wretches engaged in this appointed incendiarism were well prepared with all the appliances essential to their work. They did not need the torch. They carried with them, from house to house, pots and vessels containing combustible liquids, composed probably of phosphorus and other similar agents, turpentine, &c.; and, with balls of cotton saturated in this liquid; with which they also overspread floors and walls, they conveyed the flames with wonderful rapidity from dwelling to dwelling. Each had his ready box of Lucifer matches, and, with a scrape upon the walls, the flames began to rage. Where houses were closely contiguous, a brand from one was the means of conveying destruction to the other.

The winds favored the demons. They had been high throughout the day, and steadily prevailed from South-west by West, and bore the flames Eastward. To this fact we owe the preservation of the portions of the city lying West of Assembly street. The houses in this quarter being mostly of humble dimensions and appearance, held forth no inducements to the plunderers, and, indeed, they found sufficient employment for all their numbers in the more wealthy and fashionable portions of the city. To the abundance of the spoils in these quarters, which gave employment to all, we owe those dwellings which were saved; and possibly to this and their subsequent drunkenness, we owe the safety of our women.

XII.

The work, begun thus vigorously, went on without impediment and with hourly increase of fury throughout the night. What remained from the morning of engines and hose, were brought out by the firemen, but these were soon driven from their labors—which were indeed idle against such a storm of fire—by the pertinacious hostility of the incendiaries. Engines were tumbled over and disabled, the hose was hewn to pieces, and the firemen, dreading worse usage to themselves, left the field in despair. Meanwhile, the flames spread from side to side, from front to rear, from street to street, and where their natural and inevitable progress was too slow for the demons who had kindled them, they helped them on by the application of fresh combustibles and more rapid agencies of conflagration. By midnight, Main street, from its Northern to its Southern extremity, was a solid wall of fire. By 12 o'clock, the great blocks, which included the banking houses and the Treasury buildings, were consumed; Janney's (Congaree) and Nickerson's Hotels; the magnificent manufactories of Evans & Cogswell—indeed, every large block in the business portion of the city; the old Capitol and all the adjacent buildings were in ruins. The range called the "Granite" was beginning to flame at 12, and might have been saved by ten vigorous men, resolutely working, if there had been a will for it among the enemy or if our own firemen had been permitted. At one o'clock, the hour was struck by the clock of the Market Hall, which was even then illuminated from within. It was its own last hour which it sounded, and its tongue was silenced forevermore. In less than half an hour after, its spire went down with a crash, and, by this time, almost all the buildings within the precinct were a mass of ruins. Very grand, and terrible, beyond description, was the awful spectacle. It was a scene for the painter of the terrible. It was the blending of a range of burning mountains stretched in a continuous series for more than a mile. Here was Aetna, sending up its spouts of flaming lava; Vesuvius, emulous of like display, shooting up with loftier torrents; and Stromboli, struggling, with awful throes, to shame both by its superior volumes of fluid flame. The winds were tributary to these convulsive efforts, and tossed the volcanic torrents hundreds of feet in air. Great spouts of flame spread aloft in canopies of sulphurous cloud—wreaths of sable, edged with sheeted lightnings, wrapped the skies, and, at short intervals, the falling tower and the tottering wall, avalanche-like, went down with thunderous sound, sending up at every crash great billowy showers of glowing fiery embers.

[CONTINUED IN OUR NEXT.]

The Fire.
Main St continued. Plain to Washington—West

C A Bedell. Store, residence by Dr D P Gregg
    "   "   Central Association
J C Walker. Residence and store occupied by Dr John Ingalls
J C Walker. Store occupied by H C & H E Nichols, residence by A Feininger
J C Walker. Store occupied by P B Glass

"   Store occupied by J C Walker and Durham & Mason, Southern Baptist, second and third stories by Dr. Danelly, Southern Guardian, Masonic Hall, J B Irving, J McGown

J C Walker. Buildings on the alley occupied by Guardian Printing Office, E R
    Stokes' book bindery, Commissary stores

W B Stanley. Store

"   Rooms occupied by Confederate Treasurer, Quartermaster's Office, Commandant of Conscripts, Treasury Note Bureau, Bingham's Dancing School

Bank of the State. Bank and Branch

Independent Fire Co. Engine House

City of Columbia. Guard House

"   Market and City Hall

East.

Dr R W Gibbes and J S Guignard. Store occupied by Fisher & Agnew & Co

Gibbes and Guignard. Rooms occupied by Mrs N Scott, R Wearn's
    daguerrean gallery

Gibbes and Guignard. Store oc by A C Squier

"   "   A Falk

"   "   M A Shelton

"   "   C F Jackson

"   Dwelling occ'd by Elias Polock

"   Store oc by P W & H F Kraft

"   "   W W Walker

"   "   Com't [Commandant of] Prisoners

"   "   J G Gibbes

Com [Commisioner of] Public Buildings—Court House

Washington to Lady.—West.

R Mayrant. Residence and store occupied by L Shodair

R Mayrant. Store, etc, oc by C P Remsen

"   "   Cooper & Gaither

"   "   C D Eberhardt

J Stork. Store, house in rear oc by Prov Mar [Provost Marshall]

Henry Davis. Store, etc, oc by H Harmes

"   "   J & A Oliver

O Z Bates. Store occupied by T Stenhouse, house in rear by D Kelly and
    others

C Volger. Store occupied by L Hawley, residence by Mad [Madame] Volger

C Volger. Store oc by Treasury Department

J C Janney. Store occupied by G Stadtler
       "   "   A Feininger
Janney & Leaphart. Congaree Hotel, rooms in basement occupied by James R
    Heise and Reese's barber shop

East.

Estate C Beck. Store occupied by J C Dial
       "   P L Valory, lithographic office
       "   Commissary stores
Estate J S Boatwright. Store oc by Dr C H Miot
       "   Paymaster's office
G V Antwerp. Store occupied by J N Feaster and J C Norris, Naval Agent
       "   Residence oc by Kingman
G V Antwerp. Planter's and Mech [Mechanics] Bank
L Carr. Bank of South Carolina
       "   Rooms oc by D Wadlow and others
So Ex Co. [Southern Express Company] Store occupied by Joseph Walker
       "   "   D P McDonald
               "   Rooms oc by P Walsh and others
Dr M LaBorde. Store occupied by L T Levin
       "   Medical Purveyor's Office
G S Bower. Store oc by Bee Co, houses in rear by G S Bower
W & J Shiell. Store occupied by H Huffman
       "   "   W Shepherd
       "   "   Scott's barber shop
       "   "   H & S Beard
       "   Residence occupied by J Shiell

Lady to Gervais or Bridge.—West.

Mrs E Bailey. Store occupied by J G Forbes
       "   Residence by
       "   Store by J K Friday
       "   "   Wm Moore
Jas Hayes. Residence and store
Henry Davis. Store occupied by
       "   "   P W Kraft
W McGuinnis. Store and residence occupied by E Beraghi and D McGuinnis
W McGuinnis. Residence and store by C Brill
       "   Store occupied by Mrs P Ferguson, residence by
    Mrs C McKenna

James McKenna. Store, etc
Jacob Lyons. Commissary stores
    "   Store oc by A L Solomons
    "   "
    "   "   Muller & Senn
    "   Residence by R D Senn

East.

T S Nickerson. Nickerson's Hotel
    "   Barber shop by Wm Inglis
    "   Residence occupied by
H C Franck. Store oc by Franck & Wickenberg
T S Nickerson. Store oc by John Fanning
    "   "   Com [Commissary] State Troops
    "   "   State Ord [Ordnance] Stores
Estate R Russell. Store oc by N Winnstock
    "   "   Commissary stores
Estate B Reilly. Residence and store occupied by H Simons
Estate B Reilly. Store oc by
    "   "   P Fogarty
    "   "   P Cantwell

Gervais to Senate.

Capitol Grounds. Architect's Office, etc
    "   Sheds containing marble and granite pillars, cornices,
machinery, etc
Old Capitol

Senate to Pendleton.—West.

Mrs E J Huntt. Residence, etc

East.

Keeper Capitol. Residence oc by T Starke

Pendleton to Medium

A Palmer. Residence, etc
Jos Green (colored.) Residence

Wheat to Blossom

Mrs B Roberts. Residence
    "   Two cottages oc by

SUMTER

Upper to Richland—West

W McAlister. Blacksmith shop occupied by Kraft, Goldsmith & Kraft
Mrs Beebe. Residence
R Wearn. Residence oc by M Hislop
      "   "   Boag
M A Shelton. Residence oc by G W Logan

Richland to Laurel—West

P M Johnston. Residence oc by A T Cavis
J Oliver.   "   "   John Janes
Mrs E Law.   "   "   H Reckling

East

P G McGregor. Residence
P L Valory.   "
D B Miller.   "
J F Eisenman.   "

Laurel to Blanding—West

Estate C Beck. Residence occupied by
B Bailey.   "   Rev B M Palmer
   "   Government stables

East

C A Barnes. Residence
Presbyterian Lecture Room
A J Green. Stables, etc

Blanding to Pendleton

Mrs J Bryce. House oc by colored families
Mrs S Murphy. Dwelling, etc
Dr R W Gibbes, jr.   "
Old Baptist Church
Mrs J Friedeburg. Residence, etc
S Waddel.   "
G S Bower. Residence, etc
W F DeSaussure.   "
A C Squier.   "
Estate J S Boatwright "
J H Stelling. Residence, mill, etc

"   "   oc by J Roach and J Richard
Mrs C Neuffer. Residence, etc
F W Green. Residence oc by Miss H Bulkley
      "   Residence occupied by
W B Broom. Residence oc by C C Trumbo

UPPER

State Agricultural Society. Buildings occupied by Medical Purveyor

LUMBER

Richardson to Sumter

John McCay. Grist mill
W Riley. Residence occupied by employees of Judge's sock factory
W. Thackam. Dwelling, etc

Sumter to Marion

R. Wearn. Residence oc by T W Coogler
J Seegers.   "   A C Jacobs
Estate Miss S Ward.   "   Mrs Simons

GERVAIS

Gist to Pulaski

C C McPhail. Government Armory
Evans & Cogswell. Printing establishment

Pulaski to Lincoln

Greenville R R Co. Office, depots, etc
S C R R [South Carolina Railroad]. Depots, office, warehouses, etc
Blakely, Williams & Co. Store and wareh'e
          "   Commissary stores
Estate T Frean. Store, etc, oc by M Brown
      "   "   O'Neale & Crawford
Jas Claffey. Residence, etc

Lincoln to Gates

Estate B Reilly. Residence oc by negroes
Mrs Bailey. Residence
R O'Neale. Residence occupied by negroes
Mrs Bailey.   "   Mrs Harris
                     "   Mrs Walker
Mrs A Haight. Mary Jones

Sarah Calhoun. Residence
J Taylor. Residence oc by Julia McKean
Mrs E Glaze. Residence, etc

Assembly to Sumter

D Hane. Residence oc by a colored woman
Estate B Reilly. Dwelling, etc
T S Nickerson.　　　"
Mayor Goodwyn.　　"

Sumter to Marion

F W Green. Office oc by Nitro Bureau
　　"　　Residence, etc
J S Guignard. Residence occupied by Chan Carroll and Gen Lovell
Lecture Room of Trinity Church

Marion to Bull

Mrs B E Levy. Residence occupied by W R Taber and others

RICHLAND

Gadsden to Lincoln

State Arsenal and Academy

Richardson to Sumter

Mrs H Gill. Residence, etc

Sumter to Marion

Wm Fetner. Residence, etc
John Judge.　　　"
Lutheran Church
Jas Beard. Residence, etc

Bull to Pickens

Thos H Wade. Carpenter shop

GIST

Governm't Powder Works partially destroyed

ASSEMBLY

Richland to Laurel

Wm Elkins. Residence
H Hess. Residence oc by T B Clarkson, jr
Jas Kenneth. Residence, etc
Mrs S C Rhett. Residence oc by Maj R Rhett

Plain to Washington

J C Walker. Residence oc by T Fillette
Estate J D Kinman.　　"　　Maj Jamison
Synagogue
J T Zealy. Residence, etc

Washington to Lady

John Stork. Residence, etc
J P Southern.　　　"
G Stadtler.　　　　"
J C Janney. Livery stables

Lady to Gervais

J H Baldwin. Houses oc by colored families
[CONCLUDED IN OUR NEXT.]

COLUMBIA, S.C., SATURDAY, 25 MARCH 1865, VOL. 1, NO. 3.

XIII.

Throughout the whole of this terrible scene, the plunderers continued their ravenous search after spoil. The houses were severally and soon gutted of their contents. Hundreds of iron safes, warranted impenetrable to fire and the burglar, were not secure from the Yankee. They were split open by axes and rifled, yielding, in some cases, very largely of Confederate money and bonds, if not of gold and silver. Jewelry and plate in abundance was found. Men could be seen staggering off with huge waiters, vases, candelabra, to say nothing of cups, goblets and smaller vessels, all of solid silver. Clothes and shoes, when new, were appropriated—the rest left to burn, or tossed out into the flames. Liquors were drank with such avidity as to astonish the veteran Bacchanals of Columbia; nor did the parties thus distinguishing themselves hesitate about the vintage. There was no idle discrimination in the matter of taste, and they passed, without change of visage, from that vulgar liquor, which Judge Burke used to say always provoked within him "An inordinate propensity to sthale,"[24] to the choicest red wines of the ancient cellars. In one vault on Main street, seventeen casks of wine were stored away, which, an eye witness tells us, barely sufficed, once broken into, for the draughts of a single hour—such were the appetites at work and the numbers in possession of them. Rye, corn, claret and Madeira all found their way into the same channels, and we are not to wonder, when told that no less than 150 of the drunken wretches perished miserably among the flames kindled by their own comrades, and from which they were unable to escape. The estimate will not be thought extravagant by those who saw the condition of hundreds after 1 o'clock

A.M. By others, however, the estimate is reduced to thirty; but the number will never be known. Sherman's officers themselves are reported to have said that they lost more men in the sack and burning of the city (including certain explosions) than in all their fights while approaching it. It is also suggested that the orders which Sherman issued at daylight, on Saturday morning, for the arrest of the fire, were issued in consequence of the loss of men which he had thus sustained. One or more of his men were shot, by parties unknown, in some dark passages or alleys—it is supposed in consequence of some attempted outrages which humanity could not endure; the assassin taking advantage of the obscurity of the situation, and adroitly mingling with the crowd without. And while these scenes were at their worst—while the flames were at their highest and most extensively raging—groups of these demonics might be seen at the several corners of the streets, drinking, roaring, raging, revelling—filling the air with blasphemies—while the fiddle and accordeon were playing their popular airs among them. They executed all sorts of antics—some of them leaping in mad gyrations, and yelling and singing like the red men, around the burning pyres of their victims; brandishing knife or pistol, and in maudlin affection pawing and embracing one another, and not unfrequently the passer-by. And while these scenes were in progress, over and among the ruins already made, the torches and fireballs were busily plied in districts which had thus far escaped the flames. There was no cessation of the work till 5 A.M. on Saturday; for if one band was too drunk to play the incendiary, there were yet thousands sufficiently sober to exhibit all the skill, dexterity, agility and method which distinguishes the experts in city crime. It was between 4 and 5 in the morning, when some of the finest buildings on the East side of Main street were given to the flames.

XIV.

A single thought will suffice to show that the owners or lodgers in the houses thus sacrificed were not silent or quiet spectators of a conflagration which threw them naked and homeless under the skies of night. The male population, consisting wholly of aged men, invalids, decrepits, women and children, were not capable of very active or powerful exertions; but they did not succumb to the fate without earnest pleas and strenuous efforts. Old men and women and children were to be seen, even while the flames were rolling and raging around them, while walls were crackling and rafters tottering and tumbling, in the endeavor to save their clothing and some of their most valuable effects. It was not often that they were suffered to succeed. They were driven out headlong; pistols clapped at their heads, violent hands laid upon throat and collar, and the ruffians seemed to make but little distinction in their treatment of man or woman. Ladies were hustled from their chambers, under the strong arm, or with the menacing pistol at their breasts—their ornaments plucked from their persons, their bundles from their hands. It was in vain that the mother appealed for the garments of her children. They were torn from her grasp, and torn to pieces, or hurled into the flames. The young girl striving to save a single frock, had it rent to fibres in her grasp. Men and women bearing off their trunks were seized, despoiled, in a moment the trunk burst asunder with the stroke of axe or gun-butt, the contents laid bare, rifled of all the objects of desire, and the residue ruthlessly sacrificed to the fire; while the fiercest menaces, coupled with the foulest oaths, exhibited a desperate ferocity, such as left no hope of mercy to prayer, entreaty, and the most earnest solicitation. The wretches would lie in wait at the entrance of the house; would suffer the owner to bring forth his trunk, satisfied that he would emerge with that which was most valuable; then tear it from his grasp, with wild shouts of exultation. Scarcely one in a hundred succeeded in bearing off the poor remains of property which he had risked his life to recover. You might see the ruined owner, standing wo begone, aghast, gazing at his tumbling dwelling, his scattered property, with a dumb agony in his face that was inexpressibly touching. Others you might hear, as we did, with wild blasphemies assailing the justice of Heaven, or invoking, with lifted and clenched hands, the fiery wrath of the avenger. But the fumes plundered on, and the savage fired, and drank, and raged, and danced, and sang, and the moon sailed over all with as serene an aspect as when she first smiled upon the ark resting against the slopes of Ararat.[25]

XV.

Such was the spectacle for hours on the Main, the chief business street of Columbia. If less grand elsewhere, the spectacle was not less terrible in other portions of the city, East and West of this great centre. While thousands of the incendiaries fastened upon this part of the town, as affording to appetite the most diversified objects of plunder, the noble mansions of private citizens on fifty other squares were undergoing like horrors, at the hands of thousands more, moving in gangs and as busy at the work of plunder and destruction as those who beset the central thoroughfare. We have intimated that, at an early hour in the day, almost every house—nay, we think that there could not have been found a single exception—was visited by groups, averaging in number from two to six persons. Some of these entered civilly enough, but pertinaciously entered; in some cases, *begging* for milk, eggs, bread and meat—in most cases, demanding them. The kitchens were entered frequently by one party, while another penetrated the dwelling, and the cook was frequently astounded by the audacity by which the turkey, duck, fowl or roast was transferred from the spit to the wallet of the robber. In the house, parties less meek of temper than these pushed their way, and the first intimation of their presence, as they were confronted at the entrance, was a pistol clapped at the head or bosom of the owner, whether male or female.

"Your watch!" "Your money!" was the demand. Frequently, no demand was made. Rarely, indeed, was a word spoken, where the watch or chain, or ring or bracelet, presented itself conspicuously to the eye. It was incontinently plucked away from neck, breast or bosom, and, in some cases, the rings were torn without remorse from the bleeding ears of the woman. Hundreds of women, still greater numbers of old men, were thus despoiled. The slightest show of resistance provoked violence to the person. The venerable Mr. Alfred Huger was thus robbed in the chamber and presence of his family, and in the eye of an almost dying wife. He offered resistance, and was collared and dispossessed by violence. He told the ruffians that they would ever carry with them the degrading consciousness of being, not soldiers, but thieves and robbers. We are told that the venerable ex-Senator, Col. Arthur P. Hayne, was treated even more roughly. Mr. James Rose, besides his watch, lost largely of choice wines, which had been confided to his keeping. But we cannot descend to examples. Enough, as we have said before, that the spoils borne off from Columbia by these wretches, in the single article of gold watches, exceeded twelve hundred in number, the average value in gold being $150. Most of the more ruffianly robberies took place within the dwellings. In the open streets, the pickpockets, the experts in robbery, were mostly active. A frequent mode of operating was by first asking you the hour. If thoughtless enough to reply, producing the watch or indicating its possession, it was quietly taken from hand or pocket, and transferred to the pocket of the thief, with some such remark as this: "A pretty little watch that. I'll take it myself; it just suits me." And the appropriation followed; and if you hinted any dislike to the proceeding, a grasp was taken of your collar and the muzzle of a revolver put to your ear. Some of the incidents connected with this wholesale system were rather amusing.

Dr. Templeton, a well known and highly esteemed citizen, passing along the street, was accosted by a couple of these experts, who stopped and asked him, pointing to the arsenal building, on the hill opposite, "What building is that?" "The State arsenal," was his reply, unwisely extending his arm, as he pointed, in turn, to the building, and revealing between the folds of his coat the shining links of a rich gold chain. Before he could recover himself, his chain and watch were in the grasp of the thief, who was preparing to transfer it to his own pocket, quietly remarking, "A very pretty little watch; just to my liking." "That is very cool," said Templeton. "Just my way," said the fellow, walking off. "Stop," said Templeton, half amazed at the coolness of the proceeding, and feeling that he had only to put the best face on the matter. "Stop; that watch will be of no use to you without the key; won't you take that also?" "All right," replied the robber, returning and receiving the key.

The question, "What's o'clock?" put by a Yankee, was the sure forerunner of an attempt upon your pocket. Some parties saved their chronometers by an adroitness which deserves to be made known. One individual replied to the question, "You are too late, my good fellows. I was asked that question already by one of your parties, at the other corner." He left them to infer that the watch was already gone, and they passed him by with a curse. We are told of one person who, being thus asked for the time of day by three of them, in a street in which he could see no other of their comrades, thrust a revolver suddenly into their faces, and cocking it quickly, cried out, "Look for yourselves, you d——d scoundrels." They sheered off and left him. We, ourselves, were twice asked the question the morning after the fire, and looking innocently to where the City Hall clock once stood, replied, "Our clock is gone, you see; but it must be near 11."

Mr. J. K. Robinson was assailed with the same question by a party in the neighborhood of his house. He denied that he had a watch. "Oh! look, look!" was the answer of the questioner. "I need not look," quoth Robinson, "since I have not a watch." "Look, look a man of your appearance must own a watch." "Well, I do, but it is at home at my house." "Where's your house? We'll go and see." He took them into his house, suddenly called his guard and said, "These men are pursuing me; I know not what they want." The guard drove out the party, with successive thrusts at them of the bayonet, and from the street, defrauded of their spoils, they saluted house guard and owner with all manner of horrid execrations.

Hundreds of like anecdotes are told, not merely of loss in watches, but of every other article of property. Hats and boots, overcoats and shawls—these, when new and attractive, were sure to be taken. Even the negroes were despoiled, whenever the commodity was of any value.

The Fire.—Concluded.

LAUREL.

Between Richardson and Sumter—North.

H E and H C Nichols. Dwelling

South.

Estate C Beck. Machine shop, occupied by H Brooks

Between Sumter and Marion—North.

Dr H R Edmonds. Dwelling
S S McCully.   "
Est E B Hort.   "   oc by

Mrs Holmes. Dwelling oc by Martin and Co
     "   "   "   Mrs Fenley and others

South.

Mrs Quigley. Dwelling oc by T A Jackson
Thos Davis.   "   "   Thomas Davis and C Marshall

Between Marion and Bull—South.

Benj Evans. Dwelling.

Bull to Pickens—South.

Jacob Bell. Residence oc by Jos Manigault
Est C Beck.   "   " by Mrs C Beck and R Anderson

North.

N Ramsay. Dwelling oc by W J Laval

Richardson to Assembly—North.

G W Wright. Blacksmith shop
R Lewis. Office oc by Dr A W Kennedy
  " "   Rooms oc by Dr Kennedy, R Lewis and others

South.

Keatinge & Ball. Stables

Gates to Lincoln—North.

Glaze & Shield's Foundry

BLANDING.

Assembly to Richardson—South.

R Bryce. Warehouses

North.

M Comerford. Warehouse, etc

Richardson to Sumter.

Palmetto Engine House
Mrs Ann Marshall. Dwelling
      "   Dwelling oc by G M Johnson
B Mordecai.   "   by F G DeFontaine, Dr Baker and others

Sumter to Marion—North.

Dr A J Green. Dwelling oc Mrs Dr Ross
Mrs Z P Herndon. "   " B Mordecai

South.

Mrs John Bryce. Dwelling
C A Bedell.   "
E H Heinitsh.   "

Marion to Bull—North.

James L Clark. Residence, etc
T B Clarkson.   "

South.

Christ (Episcopal) Church
Mrs K Brevard. Residence oc W E Martin

Bull to Pickens—North.

C R Bryce. Dwelling oc Mrs McKay
    "   "   "   Harris Simons
Est C Beck.   "   "   Jas P Adams

Barnwell to Winn—South.

Mrs H English. Dwelling oc by S G Henry

North

The Charlotte Railroad passenger and freight depots, workshops, round house, etc., together with several engines and numerous cars, were destroyed; also, a quantity of printing and other material on the platforms. The dwelling house on the premises of the company, used as a boarding house for the employees, was not burnt.

TAYLOR (OR CAMDEN)
Between Harden and Laurens

E J Arthur. Residence, etc
From Mr Arthur's to Bull street nothing

Between Bull and Marion—South.

W Van Wart. Dwelling
J L Beard. Dwelling oc by H G Guerry
Est C Beck.   "   "   T W Mordecai
B J Knight.   "   "   D P McDonald
C Coogler and Miss C Daniels. Dwelling oc by Miss Daniels, Levin and others

North.

Est of Mrs Logan. Dwelling oc F A Mood
Mrs Fowle. Dwelling

Samuel Waddell. Dwelling
Mrs O M Roberts. Dwelling oc by S N Hart

Between Marion and Sumter—South

Est B Reilly. House oc by colored family
Mrs J Rawls. Dwelling oc by H D Corbett
Moses Lilienthal. Dwelling
Samuel Beard.　　　"
Benj Rawls. Dwelling oc Mrs Brightman
Mrs P B Smith.　"　"　by H Schroeder and R Duryea
Est B Reilly. Dwelling oc by H Orchard

North.

Wm Walter. Dwelling oc by John Lance
J H Carlisle.　　"　　"　Rev Jacobs
　"　"　School room oc by F W Pape
W W Walker. Dwelling
A G Goodwin.　"

Between Sumter and Richardson—South.

John Rawls. Dwelling
　"　　"　　"　oc by T D Sill
Wm H Dial. Dwelling

North.

John Veal. Dwelling
W B Stanley.　"　oc by Jos Marks
S Gardner.　"　oc by L Simons
　"　"　Office oc by Dr Davega.
H Henrichson. Dwelling
S Gardner. Telegraph Office

Between Richardson and Assembly—North.

A R Phillips. Dwelling occupied by Dr M Greenland, Mrs John Marshall,
　Mrs M Whilden, Mrs J Shingler

South.

Commercial Bank. Office oc A R Phillips
　"　　"　　"　"　Ladies' Industrial Society.
Commercial Bank. Warehouse, stables, etc, used by A R Phillips
　and others

SENATE.

Assembly to Sumter

W R Huntt. Residence occupied by Jas L Wells and W R
   Huntt

Trinity Parsonage. Rev P J Shand

Sumter to Marion

M L Brown. Residence occupied by

Marion to Bull

J S Guignard. Carpenter shops, etc

PLAIN.

Bull to Marion—South.

John H Heise. Dwelling
   "   "   "   "   oc by M H Nathan
   "   "   "   "   oc by C F Harrison
   "   "   "   "   oc Mrs G M Coffin

North

James K Friday. Dwelling
Dr J McF Gaston.   "   oc David Marks
   "   "   "   "   Unoccupied office
L W Jennings. Dwelling
Rev T E Wannamaker. Dwelling
Wm Hitchcock. Dwelling oc by J E Dent

Marion to Sumter—North.

Dr. D H Trezevant. Office and residence
Dr R W Gibbes, sr. Office filled with furn're [furnitures]
   "   "   Dwelling.

South

Jas G Gibbes. Residence oc by Dr Boozer

Sumter to Richardson—South

H Muller. Residence
Dr J W Powell. Office oc by Dr Templeton
   "   "   Residence oc by
Gibbes and Guignard. Warehouse occupied by Fisher &
   Agnew

North

Dr S Fair. Residence and office

        "   "   oc by Jos D Pepe

        "   "   Miss M Percival

        "   "   A Laughlin

        "   "   Dr E Sill

        "   "   Jas Tupper

        "   Office oc by Dr Watkins

C H Wells. Gov office oc by Maj Radcliffe

Richardson to Assembly

R C Anderson. Odd Fellows' Hall

J B Glass. Residence and Post Office

C A Bedell. Store occupied by Jas Smith

R Mayrant. Residence oc Mrs H Gladden

    "   "   "   oc by J Dobbin

  "   "   Stables

G G Newton. Paint shop

    "   "   Residence oc by W Williams

LADY

Marion to Sumter

Est I D Mordecai. Residence, etc.

Mrs J S Boatwright. Stables, etc

Richardson to Sumter.

J H Stelling. Mill, etc

John Shiell. Residence oc by W F Farley

    "   "   oc by J W and N Daniels.

John Shiell. Stables, etc

   "   Harry Nitting's bakery.

Assembly to Richardson.

J C Janney. Stables, etc

J H Baldwin. Residence

LINCOLN

E R Stokes. Dwelling and kitchen

HENDERSON

Richland to Laurel

Wm H Toy. Residence

PENDLETON

Sumter to Marion

M Brennan. Residence oc by Mrs Ferguson

WASHINGTON

Pickens to Bull

S Muldrow. Residence
C P Pelham.   "

Bull to Marion—North

D P Kelly. Residence
Methodist Parsonage. Rev W G Connor
Methodist Episcopal Church

South

Mrs G M Thompson. Residence
    "   "   "   oc by negroes
M A Shelton. Residence

Marion to Sumter

Dr A N Talley. Residence oc by Mrs A H DeLeon
    "   Office oc by L B Hanks
R L Bryan. Residence
Dr J H Boatwright. "

Sumter to Richardson

Mrs Kennerly. Residence
John Bauskett. Residence oc by J N Feaster
    "   Office oc by J Bauskett and S R Black
Law Range. Office oc by Enrolling Officer
    "   "   J D Tradewell
    "   "   F W McMaster
    "   "   W F DeSaussure
    "   "   E J Arthur
    "   "   Bachman & Waties
Brennen & Carroll. Carriage warehouse
J G Gibbes. Government warehouse
J D Bateman. Residence
F G DeFontaine & Co. South Carolinian Of
Estate C Beck. Warehouse oc by John Dial, rooms above used as Government
    Offices

Richardson to Assembly.

The District Jail.

P F Frazee. Residence oc by Mrs G Crane

   "   "   Carriage repository

   "   "   Office oc F Lance, Dr Anderson

   "   "   Residence oc by D C Peixotto

MARION

Residence oc by Clarissa May, (colored)

House oc by colored people

C H Pritchard. Residence

Lecture Room Washington Street Church

Andrew Crawford. Residence, etc

J C Lyons. Residence, etc

BULL

Geo Huggins. Residence

*** OMISSION. Richardson street. E Hunt, boarding house

Columbia, S.C., Tuesday, 28 March 1865, Vol. 1, No. 4.

XVI.

Within the dwellings, the scenes were of more harsh and tragical character, rarely softened by any ludicrous aspects. There, as it were, screened by the privacy of the apartment, with but few eyes to witness, the robbers were more brutal, more unscrupulous, less needful of decency, reserve or humanity. The pistol to the bosom or the head of woman, the patient mother, the trembling daughter, was the ordinary introduction to the demands of the robbers. "Your gold, silver, watch, jewels." They gave no time, allowed no pause or hesitation. It was in vain that the woman offered her keys, or proceeded to open drawer, or wardrobe, or cabinet, or trunk. It was dashed to pieces by axe or gun butt, with the cry, "We have a shorter way than that!" It was in vain that she pleaded to spare her furniture, and she would give up all its contents. She prayed to wretches utterly heartless in humanity, and hardened to every crime and against every human feeling. All the precious things of a family, such as the heart loves to pore on in quiet hours when alone with memory—the dear miniature, the photograph, the portrait—these were dashed to pieces, crushed under foot, and the more the trembler pleaded for, the object so precious, the more violent the rage which destroyed it. Nothing was sacred in their eyes, save the gold and silver which they bore away. Nor were these acts those of common soldiers. Commissioned officers, of rank so high as that of a colonel, were frequently among the most active in spoliation, and not always the most tender or considerate in the manner and acting of their crimes. And with fiendish malignity, refining upon hate and malice, the plunderers, after glutting themselves with spoil, would utter the foulest speeches in their ears, coupled with oaths as condiment, dealing in what they assumed, besides, to be bitter sarcasms upon their cause and country.

"And what do you think of the Yankees now?" was a frequent question. "Do you not fear us now?" "What do you think of secession?" &c., &c. "We mean to wipe you out! We'll burn the very stones of South Carolina." Even General Howard,[26] who is said to have been once a pious person, is reported to have made this reply to a citizen who had expostulated with him on the monstrous crime of which his army had been guilty: "It is only what the country deserves. It is her fit punishment; and if this does not quiet rebellion, and we have to return, we will do this work thoroughly. We will not leave woman or child."

This was in the very spirit of the savage Puritan, reviving all the brutalities of the time of Cromwell, and his sinister, psalm-singing hypocrites. The Mormonism into which New England has passed, from Puritanism, has changed none of the essential characteristics of the race.

Almost universally, the women of Columbia behaved themselves nobly under the insults of the ruffians. They preserved that patient, calm demeanor, that simple, almost masculine, firmness, which so becomes humanity in the hour of trial, when nothing can be opposed to the tempest but the virtue of inflexible endurance. They rarely replied to these insults; but looking coldly into the faces of the assailants, heard them in silence and with unblenching cheeks. When forced to answer, they did so in monosyllables only, or in brief, stern language, avowed their confidence in the cause of their country, the principles and rights for which their brothers and sons fought, and their faith in the ultimate favor and protection of God. One or two of many of these dialogues—if they may be called such, where one of the parties can urge his speech with all the agencies of power for its enforcement, and with all his instruments of terror in sight—while the other stands exposed to the worst terrors which maddened passions, insolent in the consciousness of strength—may suffice as a sample of many:

"Well, what do you think of the Yankees now?"

"Do you expect a favorable opinion?"

"No! D—n it! But you fear us, and that's enough."

"No—we do not fear you."

"What! Not yet?!"

"Not yet!"

"But you shall fear us."

"Never!"

"We'll make you."

"You may inflict, we can endure; but fear—never! Anything but that."

"We'll make you fear us!" clapping a revolver to the lady's head.

Her eye never faltered. Her cheek never changed its color. Her lips were firmly compressed. Her arms folded on her bosom. The eye of the assassin glared into her own. She met the encounter without flinching, and he lowered the implement of murder, with an oath: "D—n it! You have pluck enough for a whole regiment!"

The "pluck" of our women was especially a subject of acknowledgment with these wretches. They could admire a quality with which they had not soul to sympathize—or rather the paramount passion in their souls for greed and plunder kept in subjection all other qualities, without absolutely extinguishing them from their minds and thoughts. To inspire terror in the weak, strange to say, seemed to these creatures a sort of heroism. To extort fear and awe appeared to their monstrous vanity a tribute more grateful than any other, and a curious conflict was sometimes carried on in their minds between their vanity and cupidity. Occasionally they gave with one hand, while they robbed with another. Several curious instances of this nature took place, one of which must suffice. A certain Yankee officer happened to hear that an old acquaintance of his, whom he had known intimately at West Point and Louisiana, was residing in Columbia. He went to see him after the fire, and ascertained that his losses had been very heavy, exceeding two hundred thousand dollars. The parties had not separated for an hour, when a messenger came from the Yankee, bringing a box, which contained $100,000 in Confederate notes. This the Yankee begged his Southern friend to accept, as helping to make up his losses. The latter declined the gift, not being altogether satisfied in conscience that he could heal his own hurts of fortune by the use of stolen money. In many cases, Confederate money by the handfull was bestowed by the officers and soldiers upon parties from whom they had robbed the last particles of clothing; and even Gen. Sherman could give to parties whom he knew, the flour and bacon which he had stolen from thousands of starving widows and orphans. So, he left with the people of Columbia a hundred old worthless muskets for their protection, while emptying their arsenals of a choice collection of beautiful Enfield rifles. And so the starving citizens of Columbia owe to him a few hundred starving cattle, of which he had robbed the starving people of Beaufort, Barnwell, Orangeburg and Lexington—cattle left without food, and for which food could not be found, and dying of exhaustion at the rate of fifteen to twenty head per diem. And what a monstrous mockery of benevolence is the ostentatious contribution from navy and army, in Charleston, for the relief of those people whom their armies have so wantonly and methodically brought to ruin. They first cut our throats, then send us an adhesive plaster. The cunning of this ostentatious charity, in which they use stolen property and money, is, if possible, to persuade the world that the incendiarism which destroys all in its path is unpremeditated and purely accidental. But to return.

XVII.

In this connection and this section, in which we need to devote so much of our space to the cruel and brutal treatment of our women, we think it proper to include a communication from the venerable Dr. Sill,[27] one of the most esteemed and well known citizens of Columbia. It is from his own pen, and the facts occurred under his own eyes. We give this as one of a thousand like cases, witnessed by a thousand eyes, and taking place at the same time in every quarter of the city, almost from the hour of the enemy's arrival to that of his departure. He writes as follows:

"On Thursday, the day before the evacuation of the city by the Confederate forces, I invited a very poor French lady, (Madame Pelletier,) with her child, refugees from Charleston, to take shelter in my house, where they might, at least, have such protection as I could give her, shelter and food for herself and child. She was poor, indeed, having very little clothing and only one or two implements—a sewing machine and a crimping apparatus—by means of which she obtained a precarious support. My own family (happily) and servants being all absent, and being myself wholly incapacitated by years of sickness from making any exertion, all that the poor widow woman and myself could remove from my house, besides the few things of hers, consisted of two bags of flour, a peck of meal and about the same of grist, and about thirty pounds of bacon and a little sugar. These few things we managed to get out of the house, and, by the aid of a wheelbarrow, removed about fifty yards from the burning buildings. Waiting then and there, waiting anxiously the progress and direction of the fire, we soon found that we had been robbed of one bag of flour and a trunk of valuable books of account and papers. The fire continuing to advance on us, we found it necessary to remove again. About this time, there came up a stalwart emissary "of the best Government the world ever saw," about six feet high, accoutred with pistols, Bowie-knife, &c., and stooping down over the remaining bag of flour, demanded of the poor French lady what the bag contained. Having lost, but a few moments before, almost everything she had in the way of provisions, she seemed most deeply and keenly alive to her destitute situation, in the event she should lose the remaining bag of flour; the last and only hope of escape from starvation of her child and herself. She fell upon her knees, with hands uplifted, in a supplicating manner, and most piteously and imploringly set forth her situation to this demon in human form—an appeal which, under the circumstances, it would be impossible to conceive, more touching or heart-rending. She told him she was not here of her own choice; that herself and husband had come to Charleston in 1860 to better their fortunes; that they had been domiciled in New Jersey, where her husband had taken the necessary steps to become a citizen of the United States. She had in her hand his papers vouching the truth of her statement; that her husband had died of yellow fever in Charleston; that being unable, from want of the means, to return to New Jersey, she had been driven from Charleston to Columbia (a refugee, flying from the enemy's shells,) to try to make an honest support for herself and child. To all this, which, from its manner and matter, as I have said, was calculated to make anything short of a brute relent, he not only turned a deaf ear, but deliberately drew from his breast a huge shining Bowie knife, brandished it in her face, and with his ruffian arm, rudely pushed her aside, using, at the same time, the most menacing and obscene language; shouldered the bag of flour, and marched off, leaving the poor starving creature, with her helpless child, overwhelmed with grief and despair."

"E. Sill"

[CONTINUED IN OUR NEXT.]

Columbia, S.C., Thursday, 30 March 1865, Vol. 1, No. 5.

XVIII.

This surely is very piteous to hear, and were the case an isolated one, it would probably move compassion in every heart; but where the miseries of like and worse sort, of a whole community of twenty thousand, are massed, as it were, together before the eyes, the sensibilities become obtuse, and the universal suffering seems to destroy the sensibilities in all. We shall not seek to multiply instances like the foregoing, which would be an endless work and to little profit; and the mind of the reader can readily conceive them, when we know that Sherman dismissed his mercenaries with a general license to forage upon the people for thirty-six hours. He tells General Hampton that, could he find any civil authorities, and could they provide him with forage and provisions, he would suffer no foraging upon the people. His logic and memory are equally deficient. Was there no Mayor and Council in Columbia? They had formally surrendered the city into his hands. They constituted the civil authority; but he made no requisition upon them for provisions for his troops. He did not say to them, "Supply me with 20,000 rations in so many hours." Had he done so, the rations would have been forthcoming. The citizens would have been only too glad, by yielding up one-half of their stores, to have saved the other half, and to have preserved their dwellings from the pollution of the enemy's footsteps and presence. *Nay, did not the in-dwellers of every house—we will say 5,000 houses—seek at his hands a special guard—which usually consisted of two men—and were not these fed wholly by the families where they lodged during the whole time of their stay? Here, by a very simple computation, we find that ten thousand soldiers were thus voluntarily provided with rations;* and a requisition for twenty thousand men might easily and would prob-ably have been provided, had any such been made; for the supplies in the city were abundant of every sort—the population generally having laid in largely, and without stint or limit, anticipating a period of general scarcity from the march of the enemy. But, even had the people been unable to supply these provisions—even had the Council failed to respond to these requisitions—at whose doors should the blame be laid? The failure would have been the direct consequence of General Sherman's own proceedings. Had he not ravaged and swept, with a bosom of fire, all the tracts of country upon which the people of Columbia depended for their supplies? Had he not, himself, cut off all means of transporta-tion, in the destruction, not only of the railways, but of every wagon, cart, vehi-cle, on all the plantations through which he had passed—carrying off all the beasts of burden of any value, and ruthlessly cutting the throats of the remain-der? He cuts off the feet and arms of a people, and then demands that they shall bring him food and forage!

But even this pretext, if well grounded, can avail him nothing. *He was suffer-ing from no sort of necessity. It was the boast of every officer and soldier in his army, that he had fed fat* upon the country through which he had passed; everywhere find-ing abundance, and had not once felt the necessity of lifting the cover from his own wagons, and feeding from his own accumulated stores. The mendacity of the man strangles his logic. But the complaint of Hampton, and of our people at large, is not that he fed his followers upon the country, but that he destroyed what he did not need for food, and tore the bread from the famishing mouths of a hundred thousand women and children—feeble infancy and decrepit age; and this, too, coupling with the robbery and incendiarism, deeds of the foulest vio-lence, the most reckless debauchery, the meanest practices of thief and outlaw. But to our narrative.

XIX.

We have adverted to the deeper black of those horrid outrages which were per-petrated within the households of the citizen, where, unrestrained by the rebuk-ing eyes of their own comrades, and unresisted by their interposition; cupidity, malignity and lust, sought to glut their several appetites. The cupidity generally triumphed over the lust. The greed for gold and silver swallowed up the more animal passions, and drunkenness supervened in season for the safety of many. We have heard of some few outrages, or attempts at outrage, of the worst sort, but the instances, in the case of white females, must have been very few. There

was, perhaps, a wholesome dread, on the part of the ruffians, of goading to des-
peration the people whom they had despoiled of all but honor. They could see,
in many watchful and guardian eyes, the lurking expression which threatened
sharp vengeance should their trespasses proceed to those extremes which they
yet unquestionably contemplated. The venerable Mr. H. stood ready, with his
couteau de chasse, made bare in his bosom, hovering around the persons of his
innocent daughters. Mr. O., on beholding some too familiar approach to one of
his daughters by one of the ruffians, bade him stand off at the peril of his life;
saying that, while he submitted to be robbed of property, he would sacrifice life
without reserve—his own and that of the assailant—before his child's honor
should be abused. Mr. James G. Gibbes with difficulty, pistol in hand, and only
with the assistance of a Yankee officer, rescued two young women from the
clutches of as many ruffians. We have been told of successful outrages of this
unmentionable character being practiced upon women dwelling in the suburbs.
Many are understood to have taken place in remote country settlements, and
two cases are described where young negresses were brutally forced by the
wretches and afterwards murdered—one of them being thrust, when half dead,
head down, into a mud puddle, and there held until she was suffocated. But this
must suffice. The shocking details should not now be made, but that we need,
for the sake of truth and humanity, to put on record, in the fullest types and
columns, the horrid deeds of these marauders upon all that is pure and precious
—all that is sweet and innocent—all that is good, gentle, gracious, dear and
ennobling—within the regards of white and Christian civilization. And yet, we
should grossly err if, while showing the forbearance of the Yankees in respect to
our *white* women, we should convey to any innocent reader the notion that they
exhibited a like forbearance in the case of the *black*. The poor negroes were terribly victimized by their brutal assailants, many of them, besides the instance
mentioned, being left in a condition little short of death. Regiments, in successive *relays*, subjected scores of these poor women to the torture of their em-
braces, and—but we dare not farther pursue the subject—it is one of such
loathing and horror. There are some horrors which the historian dare not pursue—which the painter dare not delineate. They both drop the curtain over
crimes which humanity bleeds to contemplate.[28]

Some incidents of gross brutality, which show how well prepared were these
demons for every crime, however monstrous, may be given.

A lady, undergoing the pains of labor, had to be borne out on a mattress into
the open air, to escape the fire. It was in vain that her situation was described to
the incendiaries, as they applied the torch within and without the house, after they
had penetrated every chamber and robbed them of all that was either valuable or

portable. They themselves beheld the situation of the sufferer, and laughed to scorn the prayer for her safety.

Another case was that of Mrs.——, a widow. Her corpse, decked for the grave, was surrounded by watchful mourners, sisters and daughters. Into this sacred presence the ruffians made their way, plundering as they went, making offensive comments, and exhibiting no sort of regard to the solemn preparations for the grave which they beheld, or for the bereaved sufferers, silent in their sad offices of love.

Another lady, Mrs. J——, was but recently confined. Her condition was very helpless. Her life hung upon a hair. The demons were apprised of all the facts in the case. They burst into the chamber—took the rings from the lady's fingers—plucked the watch from beneath her pillow—shrieked offensive language in her ears, and so overwhelmed her with terror, that she sunk under the treatment—surviving their departure but a day or two. Language fails in all adequate speech, when it would properly characterize the nature of these demons or their diabolical performances.

In several cases, newly made graves were opened, the coffins taken out, broken open, in search of buried treasure, and the corpses left exposed. Every spot in grave yard or garden, which seemed to have been recently disturbed, was sounded with sword, or bayonet, or ramrod, in their desperate search after spoil. These monsters of virtuous pretension, with their banner of streaks and spangles overhead, and sworn to the Constitution, which they neither understand nor read, never once forget the greed of appetite which has distinguished Puritanic New England for three hundred years; and, lest they might forget, the appetite is kept lively by their women—letters found upon their dead, or upon prisoners, almost invariably appealing to them to bring home the gauds and jewelry, even the dresses, of the Southern women, to deck the fond feminine expectants at home, whom we may suppose to be all the while at their devotions, assailing Heaven with prayer in behalf of their thrice blessed cause and country.

[CONTINUED IN OUR NEXT.]

COLUMBIA, S.C., SATURDAY, 1 APRIL 1865, VOL. 1, NO. 6.

XX.

In this grave connection, we have to narrate a somewhat picturesque transaction, less harsh of character and less tragic, and preserving a somewhat redeeming aspect to the almost uniform brutality of our foes. Mr. Melvin M. Cohen[29] had a guard given him for his home, who not only proved faithful to their trust, but showed themselves gentle and unobtrusive. Their comrades, in large numbers, were encamped on the adjoining and vacant lands. These latter penetrated his grounds, breaking their way through the fences, and it was not possible, where there were so many, to prevent their aggression entirely. The guard kept them out of the dwelling, and preserved its contents, and this was much. They were not merely civil, but amused the children of the family; played with them, sympathized in their fun, and contributed to their little sports in sundry ways. The children owned a pretty little pet, a grey-hound, which was one of the most interesting of their sources of enjoyment. The soldiers, without, seemed to remark at the play of the guard with the children and dog with discontent and displeasure. They gave several indications of a morose temper in regard to them, and, no doubt, they considered the guard with hostility, per se, as guard, and because of their faithful protection of the family. At length, their displeasure prompted one of them to take an active but cruel part in the pastimes of the children. This wretch, gathering up a stone, watched his moment, and approaching the group, where they were at play, suddenly dashed out the brains of the little dog, at the very feet of the children. They were terribly frightened, of course, at this cruel exhibition of power and malignity. Their grief followed in bitter lamentations and tears. To soothe them, the soldiers of the guard took up the remains of the dog, dug for it a grave in one of the flower beds of the garden, tenderly laid it in the earth, and raised a mound over it, precisely as if it had been a human child. A stake at the head and feet rendered the proceeding complete.

That night, Mr. Cohen returning home, his wife remarked to him:

"We have lost our silver. It was buried in the very spot where these men have buried the dog. They, have no doubt found it, and it is lost to us."

It was impossible then to attempt any search for the relief of their anxiety, until the departure of the marauders. When they had gone, however, the search was eagerly made, and the buried treasure found untouched. But the escape was a narrow one. The cavity made for the body of the dog approached within a few inches the box of silver.

Mayor Goodwyn also saved a portion of his plate through the fidelity of his guard. But he lost his dwelling and everything besides. We believe that, in every instance where the guard proved faithful, they were Western men. They professed to revolt at the spectacles of crime which they were compelled to witness, and pleaded the necessity of a blind obedience to orders, in justification of their share of the horrors to which they lent their hands. Just before the conflagration began; about the dusk of evening, while the Mayor was conversing with one of the Western men, from Iowa, three rockets were shot up by the enemy from the capitol square. As the soldier beheld these rockets, he cried out:

"Alas! Alas! for your poor city! It is doomed. Those rockets are the signal. The town is to be fired."

In less than twenty minutes after, the flames broke out in twenty distinct quarters.

XXI.

Of the conflagration itself, we have already given a sufficient idea, so far as words may serve for the description of a scene which beggars, art and language to portray. We have also shown, in some degree, the usual course of proceeding among the incendiaries; how they fired the dwelling as they pillaged; how they abused and outraged the indwellers; how they mocked at suffering, scorned the pleadings of women and innocence, and ruthlessly persevered in their demonic cruelties, though at the peril of life to the invalid and weak. As the flames spread from house to house, you could behold, through long vistas of the lurid empire of flames and gloom, the miserable tenants of the once peaceful home issuing forth in dismay, bearing the chattels most useful or precious, and seeking escape through the narrow channels which the flames left them only in the centre of the streets. Fortunately, the streets of Columbia are very wide, and greatly protected by umbrageous trees, set in regular order, and which, during the vernal season, confer upon the city one of its most beautiful features. But for this width of its passages, thousands must have been burned to death. These families moved in long procession, the aged sire or grand-sire first—a sad, worn and tottering man; walking steadily on, with rigid, set features and tearless eyes—too much stricken, too much stunned, for any ordinary shows of suffering. Perhaps, the aged wife hung upon one arm, while the other was supported by a daughter. And huddling close, like terrified partridges, came the young, each bearing some little bundle —all pressing forward under the lead of the sire, and he witless where to go. The ascending fire spouts flamed before them on every hand—the shouts of the demonics assailed them at every step—the infernal furies danced around them as they went, piercing their ears with horrid threats and imprecations. The little bundles were snatched from the grasp of their trembling bearers, torn open, sacked, and what did not tempt the robber was hurled into the contiguous pile of flame. And group after group, stream after stream, of fugitives thus pursued their way through the paths of flaming and howling horror, only too glad to fling themselves on the open ground, whither, in some cases, they had succeeded in conveying a feather bed or mattress. The malls, or open squares, the centres of the wide streets, like Empress street,[30] were thus strewn with piles of bedding, on which lay exhausted mothers—some of them with anxious physicians in attendance, and girdled by crouching children, and infants, wild and almost idiotic with their terrors. In one case, as we have mentioned, a woman about to become a mother was thus borne out from a burning dwelling. It was scarcely possible to advise in which direction to fly. The churches were at first sought by many several streams of population. But these were found to afford no security. Thither the hellish perseverance of the fiends followed them, and the churches of God were set on flame. Again driven forth, numbers made their way into the recesses of Sidney Park, and here fancied to find security, as but few houses occupied the neighborhood, and these not sufficiently high to lead to apprehension from the flames. But the ingenuity of hate and malice was not to be baffled, and fire-balls, thrown from the heights into the deepest hollows of the park, taught the wretched fugitives to despair of any refuge from enemies of such unwearied and unremitting rage. Again were they forced to scatter, finding their way to other places of retreat, and finding none of them secure.

XXII.

One of these mournful processions of fugitives was that of the sisterhood of the Convent, the nuns and their pupils. Beguiled to the last moment by the specious promises and assurances of officers and others in Sherman's army, the Mother Superior had clung to her house to the last possible moment. It was not merely a home, but in some degree a temple; and, to the professors of one church at least, a shrine. It had been chosen, as we have seen, as the place of refuge for many of other churches. We have already assigned the reasons which led all parties to believe that it was particularly safe as a retreat. Much treasure had been lodged in it for safe keeping, and the Convent had a considerable treasure of its own. It was liberally and largely furnished, not only as a domain, but as an academy of the highest standard. It was complete in all the agencies and material for such an academy and for the accommodation of perhaps two hundred pupils. Among these agencies for education were no less than seventeen pianos. The harp, the guitar, the globe, the maps, desks, benches, bedding and clothing, were all supplied on a scale of equal amplitude. The establishment also possessed some fine pictures, original and from the first masters. The removal of these was impossible, and hence the reluctance of the Mother Superior to leave her house was sufficiently natural. Assured, besides of safety, she remained until further delay would have perilled the safety of her innocent and numerous flock. This lady marshalled her procession with great good sense, coolness and decision. They were instructed to secure the clothes most suitable to their protection from the weather, and to take with them those valuables which were portable; and, accompanied by the Rev. Dr. O'Connell, by Mr. Jacob Cohen[31] who was especially efficient in their service—and others, the damsels filed on, under the lead of their Superior, through long tracts of fire, burning roofs, tumbling walls, wading through billows of flame, and taking, at first, the pathway to St. Peter's (Catholic) Church. Blinding fires left them almost aimless in their march; but they succeeded in reaching the desired point in safety. Here, on strips of bedding, quilts and coverlets, the young girls found repose, protected by the vigilance of a few gentlemen, their priest, Mr. Cohen,[32] and we believe by two officers of the Yankee army, whose names are given as Col. Corley and Dr. Galaghan. To these gentlemen, both Catholic Irish, the Mother Superior acknowledges her great indebtedness. They had need of all the watch and vigilance of these persons. It was soon found that the fiends had followed them in their flight, like sleuth-hounds, and were making attempts to fire the edifice on several sides. These attempts, repeatedly baffled and as often renewed, showed at length so tenacious a purpose for its destruction, that it was thought best to leave the building and seek refuge in the church-yard, and there, in the cold and chill, and among the grave-stones with the dead, these terrified living ones, denied to rest, remained, trembling watchers through the rest of this dreary night.

XXIII.

We take leave here, to borrow freely from communication made by the Rev. Lawrence P. O'Connell to the Catholic *Pacificator.* He so fully reports the fate of St. Mary's College that nothing need be added to it. We have simply abridged such portions of his statement as might be dispensed with in this connection:

"St. Mary's College, founded in 1852 by the Rev. J. J. O'Connell, pastor of the Catholics in Columbia, was robbed, pillaged and then given to the flames. The College was a very fine brick building, and capable of accommodating over one hundred students. It had an excellent library attached, which was selected with great care, and with no limited view to expense. It also possessed several magnificent paintings, executed in Rome, and presented to the institution by kind patrons. Besides the property belonging to St. Mary's College, that of four priests, who were its professors and lived there, was also consumed. Each, as is always the case amongst the Catholic clergy, had his individual collection of books, paintings, statuary, sacred pictures, &c. Nobody who is not a rigorous student and a lover of literature can possibly realize the losses sustained by these gentlemen. Manuscripts of rare value, notes taken from lectures of the most eminent men in Europe and America, orations, sermons, &c, are treasures not often valued by the vulgar, but to the compiler they are more priceless than diamonds. Of those who lost all in St. Mary's, three are brothers, viz: Revs. Jeremiah J. O'Connell, Lawrence P. O'Connell, and Joseph P. O'Connell, D.D.; and the other, Rev. Augustus J. McNeal."

The Post Chaplain, the author of the report from which we draw, was the only clergyman in the College when it was destroyed. He was made a prisoner, and though pleading to be allowed to save the holy oils, &c., his prayer was rejected with blasphemies and curses. A sacrilegious squad drank their whiskey from the sacred chalice. The sacred vestments and consecrated vessels used for the celebration of the mass—all things, indeed, pertaining to the exercise of sacerdotal function—were profaned and stolen. Of the College itself, and the property which it contained, nothing was saved but the massed ruins, which show where the fabric stood. The clergymen saved nothing beyond the garments which they had upon their persons.

XXIV.

The destruction of private libraries and valuable collections of objects of art and virtu, was very large in Columbia. It was by the urgent entreaties of the Rev. Mr. Porter,[33] the professors and others, that the safety of the South Carolina College library was assured. The buildings were occupied by Confederate hospitals, where some three hundred invalids and convalescents found harborage. The yellow flag would have proved but little protection for them, but for the efforts of these gentlemen, and, perhaps, because of other considerations. They held forth no promise of plunder, were remote from those parts of the city where the temptations were most numerous, and the professors of colleges are not usually hoarders, or even gentlemen of gold and silver vessels. These generally occupied the dwellings of the College; they escaped with some petty losses. Professor John LeConte was made a prisoner and carried off; but why he was selected thus, is not very apparent. After a few days in durance, he was suffered to depart, and left the army on its march. In a conversation with the Rev. Mr. Porter regarding the safety of the College library, General Sherman indulged in a sneer; "I would rather," said he, "give you books than destroy them. I am sure your people need them very much." To this Mr. Porter made no reply, suffering the eloquent General to rave for awhile, upon a favorite text with him, the glories of his flag and the perpetuation of the Union, which he solemnly pledged himself to maintain, against all the fates.

That his own people did not value books, in any proper degree, may be shown by their invariable treatment of libraries. These were almost universally destroyed, tumbled into the weather, the streets, gutters, hacked and hewn and trampled, even when the collections were of the rarest value and in immense numbers. Libraries of ten thousand volumes—books such as cannot again be procured—were sacrificed in the hope of procuring a few hundred dollars worth of plunder. It will suffice to illustrate the numerous losses of this sort in Columbia, to report the fate of the fine collections of Dr. R. W. Gibbes. This gentleman, a man of letters and science, a virtuoso, busied all his life in the accumulation of works of art and literature, and rare objects of interest to the amateur and student, has been long known to the American world, North and South, in the character of a savant. Perhaps no other person in South Carolina has more distinguished himself by his scientific writings, and by the indefatigable research which illustrated them, by the accumulation of proofs from the natural world. A friendly correspondent gives us a mournful narrative of the disasters to his house, his home, his manuscripts and his various and valuable collections, from which we condense the following particulars:

"Besides the fine mansion of Dr. Gibbes and its usual contents of furniture, his real estate on Main street, &c., his scientific collections and paintings were of immense value, occasioning more regret than could arise from any loss of mere property. His gallery contained upwards of two hundred paintings, among which were two pictures by Washington Allston, of inestimable value; several by Sully and Inman, and many admirable landscapes by Charles Fraser. The earliest and latest works of DeVeaux constituted treasures of infinite value, which the future would have rejoiced to study; and many originals and copies, by European hands, were highly prized from their intrinsic excellence and interesting associations—each having its own history. There was an original portrait of Garrick, by Pine, and one of the "Seven Ages" of Shakspeare [*sic*], painted for Alderman Boydell; there were portraits of Washington Allston, Gen. Z. Taylor, Col. Wade Hampton—all friends of the proprietor, and from the hands of the best artists. The family portraits in the collection were also numerous—some ancient, all valuable; and several admirable busts graced his drawing room. His portfolios contained collections of the best engravings from the most famous pictures of the old masters and by the most excellent engravers of the age. These were mostly a bequest from the venerable C. Fraser, who was one of those who best knew what a good engraving or picture should be, and who had, all his life, been engaged in accumulating the most valuable illustrations of the progress of art. Nor was the library of Dr. G. less rich in stores of letters and science, art and medicine. His historical collection was particularly rich, especially in American and South Carolina history. His cabinet of Southern fossils and memorials, along with those brought from the remotest regions, was equally select and extensive. It contained no less than ten thousand specimens. The collection of shark's teeth was pronounced by Agassiz to be the finest in the world. His collections of historical documents, original correspondence of the Revolution, especially that of South Carolina, was exceedingly large and valuable. From these he had compiled and edited three volumes, and had there arrested the publication, in order to transfer his materiel to the Historical Society of South Carolina. All are now lost. So, also, was his collection of autographs—the letters of eminent correspondents in every department of letters, science and art. Many relics of our aborigines, others from the pyramids and tombs of Egypt, of Herculanenm, Pompeii and Mexico, with numerous memorials from the Revolutionary and recent battle-fields of our country, shared the same fate—are gone down to the same abyss of ruin. The records of the Surgeon General's

Department of the State, from its organization, no longer exist. The dwelling which contained these inestimable treasures was deliberately fired by men, for whose excuse no whiskey influence could be pleaded. They were quite as sober as in a thousand other cases where they sped with the torch of the incendiary. It was fired in the owner's presence, and when he expostulated with them, he was laughed to scorn. A friend who sought to extinguish the fire kindled in his very parlor, was seized by the collar and hurled aside, with the ejaculation, "Let the d——d house burn."

[CONTINUED IN OUR NEXT.]

COLUMBIA, S.C., TUESDAY, 4 APRIL 1865, VOL. 1, NO. 7.

XXV.

It was one almost invariable feature of the numerous melancholy processions of fugitive women and children and old men escaping from their burning houses, to be escorted by Yankee officers or soldiers—as frequently by the one as by the other—who sometimes pretended civility; and mixed it up with jeering or offensive remarks upon their situation. These civilities had an ulterior object. To accept them, under the notion that they were tendered in good faith, was to be robbed or insulted. The young girl carrying work-box or bundle, who could be persuaded to trust it to the charge of one of those creatures, very often lost possession of it wholly.

"That trunk is small, but it seems heavy," quoth one to a young lady, who in the procession of the nuns, was carrying off her mother's silver. "What's in it, I wonder? Let me carry it." "No, thank you. My object is to save it, if I can." "Well, I'll save it for you; let me help you." "No, I need no help of yours, and wish you to understand that I mean to save it, if I can." "You are too proud, miss! but we'll humble you yet. You have been living in clover all your life—we'll bring you down to the wash-tub. Those white hands shall be done brown in the sun before we're done with you," &c. There spoke out that Yankee envy at Southern prosperity and the superior privileges of our civilization, which lurks at the bottom of the Yankee heart, which has shown itself in a thousand forms of spite, ill-feeling and malice, for thirty years, and now reaches its climax in robbery, incendiarism and massacre. It is not surprising to those who have long known the characteristics of this people, that their officers, even ranking as high as colonels, were found as active in the work of insults and plunder as any of their common men. One of these colonels came into the presence of a young girl, a pupil at the Convent, and the daughter of a distinguished public man. He wore in his hat her riding plume, attached by a small golden ornament, and in his hands he carried her riding whip. She calmly addressed him thus: "I have been robbed, sir, of every article of clothing and ornaments; even the dress I wear is borrowed. I am resigned to their loss. But there are some things that I would not willingly lose. You have in your cap the plume from my riding hat—you carry in your hand my riding whip. They were gifts to me from a precious friend. I demand them from you." "Oh! these cannot be yours—I have had them a long time." "You never had them before last night. It was then I lost them. They are mine, and the gold ornament of the feather engraved with the initials of the giver. Once more I demand them of you." "Well, I'm willing to *give* them to you, if you'll accept them as a keep sake." "No, sir, I wish no keep-sake of yours; I shall have sufficiently painful memories to remind me of those whom I could never willingly see again—whom I have never wished to see." "Oh! I rather guess you're right there," with a grin. "Will you restore me my whip and feather?" "As a keep sake! Yes." "No, sir, as my property, which you can only wear as stolen property." "I tell you, if you'll take them as a keep-sake from me, you shall have them." "You must then keep them, sir—happy, perhaps, that you cannot blush whenever you sport the plume or flourish the whip." And the miserable wretch, representative of the best Government and the most saintly people of the world, bore off the stolen treasures of the damsel.

In these connections, oaths of the most blasphemous kind were rarely foreborne, even when their talk was had with females. They had a large faith in Sherman's generalship. One of their lieutenants is reported to have said: "He's all hell at flanking. He'd flank God Almighty out of Heaven and the devil into hell!"

XXVI.

But this is enough on this topic, and we must plead the exactions of truth and the necessities of historical evidence, to justify us in repeating and recording such monstrous blasphemies. We shall hereafter, from other hands, be able to report some additional dialogues held with the women of Columbia, by some of the Yankee officers. Of their temper, one or two more brief anecdotes will suffice.

The Convent, among its other possessions, had a very beautiful model of the Cathedral, of Charleston. This occupied a place in the Convent ground. It was destroyed by the soldiers. One of the nuns lamented its fate to the Mother Superior, in the presence of Col. Ewell [?],[34] an aid of one of the generals. He muttered bitterly, "Yes, it is rightly served; and I could wish the same fate to befall every cathedral in which Te Deum has been performed at the downfall of our glorious flag."

A gentleman was expressing to one of the Yankee Generals the fate of the Convent, and speaking of the losses, especially of the Lady Superior. He replied dryly: "It is not forgotten that this lady is the sister of Bishop Lynch, who had Te Deum performed in his cathedral at the fall of Fort Sumter."

A lady of this city spoke indignantly to Gen. Atkins, of Sherman's army, and said of that General, "He wars upon women!" "Yes," said Atkins, "and justly. It is the women of the South who keep up this cursed rebellion. It gave us the greatest satisfaction to see those proud Georgia women begging crumbs from Yankee leavings; and this will soon be the fate of all of you Carolina women."

A few more samples of the sort of talk which they held with our people, especially the women, will serve to illustrate more completely the cold-blooded, viperous and thoroughly base character of the invaders, while showing the spirit of our women under this cruel ordeal.

Escorting a sad procession of fugitives from the burning dwellings, one of them said: "What a glorious sight!" "Terribly so," said one of the ladies. "Grand!" said he. "Very pitiful," was the reply. The lady added: "How, as men, you can behold the horrors of this scene and behold the sufferings of these innocents, without terriblest pangs of self-condemnation and self-loathing, it is difficult to conceive." "We glory in it!" was the answer. "I tell you, madam, that when the people of the North hear of the vengeance we have meted out to your city, there will be one universal shout of rejoicing from man, woman and child, from Maine to Maryland." "You are, then, sir, only a fitting representative of your people."

Another said to a group of ladies, while escorting them, on a similar flight from the fire, and timing their progress by like sneers and sarcasms: "You needed illumination here. You see on what a grand scale we make ours." "Yes, you have kindled such torches as will need all the blood in all your veins to extinguish. You exult now, but could you foresee! When you march hence, you will go to retribution."

Another, who had thus forced himself as an escort upon a party, on the morning of Saturday, said, pointing to the thousand stacks of chimneys, "You are a curious people here in house-building. You run up your chimneys before you build the house."

One who had been similarly impudent, said to a mother, who was bearing a child in her arms, "Let me carry the baby, madam." "Do not touch him for your life," was the reply. "I would sooner hurl him into the flames and plunge in after him than that he should be polluted by your touch. Nor shall a child of mine ever have even the show of obligation to a Yankee!" "Well, that's going it strong, by ——, but I like your pluck. We like it, d——e; and you'll see us coming back after the war—every man of us—to get a Carolina wife. We hate your men like h——, but we love your women!" "We much prefer your hate, even though it comes in fire! Will you leave us, sir!"

It was not always, however, that our women were able to preserve their coolness and firmness under the assaults of the brutes who encountered them. We have quite an amusing story of a luckless wife, who was confronted by a stalwart ruffian, with a horrid oath and a cocked revolver at her head, "Your watch! your money! you d—d rebel b——h!" The horrid oaths, the sudden demand, fierce look and rapid action, so terrified her that she cried out, "Oh! my G—! I have no watch, no money, except what's tied round my waist!" We need not say how deftly the robber applied his Bowie-knife to loose the stays of the lady. She was then taught, for the first time in her life, that the stays were wrongly placed. They should have been upon her tongue.

In all their conversation, the officers exhibited the usual swelling, inflated, bombastic manner, and their exaggerations of their strength and performances were amusingly great and frequent. On their first arrival, they claimed generally to have 60,000 men; in a few hours after, the number was swollen to 75,000; by night, it had reached 100,000; and on Saturday, the day after, they claimed to have 125,000. We have already estimated the real number at 40,000—total cavalry, infantry and artillery.

[CONTINUED IN OUR NEXT.]

COLUMBIA, S.C., THURSDAY, 6 APRIL 1865, VOL. 1, NO. 8.

XXVII.

We have already passingly adverted to the difficulty of saving the South Carolina College library from the flames, and lest we should have conveyed a false impression in respect to the degree of effort made in saving it, we give some particulars which may be found of interest. We need scarcely say that the professors clung to their sacred charge with a tenacity which never once abandoned it or forebore the exertions necessary for its safety; while the officers of the several hospitals, to which the College buildings were generally given up, were equally prompt to give their co-operation. Very soon after the entrance of the enemy into the city, Dr. Thompson, of the hospital, with Professors LaBorde, Reynolds and Rivers,[35] took their places at the gate of the College Campus, and awaited their approach. Towards noon, a body of Yankees, led by a Captain Young, made their appearance at the gate, and the surgeon, with the professors, made a special appeal to the captain for the protection of the library and the College buildings; to which he replied with a solemn assurance that the place should be spared, and that he would station a sufficient guard within and without the walls. He remarked, with some surprise, upon the great size of the enclosure and establishment. The guard was placed, and no serious occasion for alarm was experienced throughout the day; but, from an early hour of the night, the buildings began to be endangered by showers of sparks from contiguous houses, which fell upon their roofs. This danger increased hour by hour, as the flames continued to advance, and finally, the roofs of the several dwellings of Professors LaBorde and Rivers burst out in flames. Their families were forced to fly, and it required all the efforts of professors, surgeons, servants, even aided by a file of the Yankees, to arrest the conflagration. Every building within the campus was thus in danger, and Professor Reynolds spent most of the night upon his roof, in order to secure its safety. The destruction of any one building would to a certainty have led to the loss of all. The most painful apprehensions were quickened into a sense of horror, when the feeble inmates of the hospital were remembered. There were numbers of noble soldiers, brave Kentuckians and others, desperately wounded, to whom—lacking, as the establishment did at that moment, the necessary labor—but little assistance could be rendered. They were required to shift for themselves, while the few able-bodied men within the campus were on the house tops fighting the fire. The poor fellows were to be seen dragging their maimed and feeble bodies, as best they could, along the floors, adown the stairs, and crawling out, with great pain and labor, and by the tardiest process, into that atmosphere of reeking flame, which now girdled the establishment. Others, again, unable to leave their beds, resigned themselves to their fate. We can better conceive than describe the terrible agonies, to them, of those hours of dreadful anticipation in which they lay. Happily, the fires were subdued by 4 in the morning of Saturday.

But the danger, even then, was not over. About 8 A.M., the College gate was assaulted by a band of drunken cavalry, 150 or more, savage, infuriate, bent upon penetrating the campus, and swearing to fire the buildings. The officer in command of the guard reported to the professors that his force was not adequate to the protection of the establishment, and that he was about to be overwhelmed. Professors LaBorde and Rivers, followed by Surgeon Thompson, at once sped, in all haste, to the headquarters of Gen. Howard, appealing to him, in the most passionate terms, to redeem his pledge for the protection of the College and its library. He promptly commanded his Chief of Staff, Col. Stone, to repair to the scene and arrest the danger. This—revolver in hand—he promptly did, and succeeded in dispersing the incendiary cavalry.

It may not be out of place to mention that Professors LaBorde, Reynolds and Rivers were the only members of the Faculty present during the invasion of the Yankee hordes. Professor LeConte was not captured within the city, but while in Confederate service, at several miles distance.

It is with profound regret that we add that the Legislative library, consisting of 25,000 choice volumes, was wholly destroyed in the old Capitol.

XXVIII.

Among the moral and charitable institutions which suffered greatly in the fire, were the several Masonic[36] bodies. They lost everything, with rare exceptions:

houses, lodges, regalias, charts, charters, jewels, and every form of implement and paraphernalia. Much of this property had been accumulated in Columbia from Charleston and other places—had been sent hither for safe keeping. Their losses will for a long while be wholly irreparable, and cannot be repaired, unless, indeed, through the liberality of remote and wealthy fraternities in other sections. The furniture and jewels were, in the largest number of cases, of the richest and most valuable order, wholly of silver, and in great proportion were gifts and bequests of favorite brothers who had reached the highest ranks in the order. We enumerate the following lodges as the chief sufferers:

1. Richland Lodge No. 39, A. F. M.
2. Acacia Lodge No. 94, A. F. M.
3. True Brotherhood Lodge No. 84, A. F. M.

[These all met in Columbia.]

4. Union Kilwinning No. 4, A. F. M.
5. Orange No. 14, A. F. M.

[These met in Charleston.]

6. Carolina Chapter No. 1, R. A. M.
7. Columbia Chapter No. 5, R. A. M.
8. Union Council No. 5, R. A. M.
9. Enoch Lodge of Perfection—Ineffable degrees.
10. DeMolay Council, Knights of Kadosch—Ineffable degrees.

The Independent Order of Odd Fellows and other orders were sufferers in like degree with the Masonic bodies. These were:

1. Palmetto Lodge No. 5.
2. Congaree Lodge No. 29.
3. Eutaw Encampment Lodge No. 2.
4. Sons of Temperance.
5. Sons of Malta.

The buildings, chambers, and lodges which contained the treasures of these bodies, were first plundered and then given to the flames. The soldiers were to be seen about the streets, dressed up in the aprons, scarfs and regalias. Some of the Yankee Masons were active in endeavoring to arrest the robbers in their work, but without success. In a conversation with one of the Western Masons, he responded to the signs and behaved courteously, but he said: "We are told that all fraternization with your Masonic bodies of the South, has been cut off, in consequence of your Masons renouncing all connection or tie between them and the Masons of the North." We replied to him that the story was absurd, and evidently set afloat in order to prevent the *Northern* Masons from affording succor to a Southern brother in the hour of his distress—that Masonry overrides the boundaries of States, allows of no political or religious differences, and that its very nature and constitution are adverse to the idea of any such renunciations of the paramount duties of the craft, in all countries and under all circumstances.

We add a few particulars in relation to some of these lodges, showing the extent and character of their losses. The minutes of Union Kilwinning Lodge No. 4, were more than a century old; those of Lodge No. 14, very near a century. These are all gone, and the loss is irremediable. A portion of the minutes of Richland Lodge No. 39, are supposed to be safe, as they were confided to the keeping of a Masonic writer, with a view to the preparation of a history. He will probably, from this notice, perceive the propriety of restoring them to the Lodge as soon as possible.

XXIX.

Among the items of loss, which are particularly lamented, that of the famous sword of State, called "the Cromwell Sword," belonging to the Grand Lodge of South Carolina, is particularly deplored. This was an antique of peculiar interest and value. Its history, as given by Dalcho, may be given here, as particularly calculated to gratify the curious, as well as the Masonic reader. It was a large, elegant and curious two-edged weapon, in a rich velvet scabbard, highly ornamented with Masonic emblems, and with the arms of the Grand Master. It had been presented to the Grand Lodge by the Provincial Grand Master, after the installation of the grand officers, was given as a consecrated sword, and received with reverent assurances, to keep it safely, so far as human effort could accord safety. The weapon had been long in the possession of the Grand Master's family, and was said to have once belonged to Oliver Cromwell, a legend to which some degree of probability may be given, from the fact that the Provincial Grand Master was a descendant of Sir Edward Leigh, who was a member of the Long Parliament and a Parliamentary General in the time of the Protector, from whom, perhaps, he received it.

The farther history of this sword may as well be given here. From the time of the presentation it continued in the possession of the Grand Lodge, and was borne by the Grand Sword Bearer, or in later times, the Grand Pursuivant, in all public processions. At length, at the conflagration which, in the year 1838, destroyed so large a portion of the city of Charleston, and with other buildings the Masonic Hall, the sword was, with great difficulty, saved by brother Samuel Seyle, the Grand Tiler, with the loss of the hilt, the scabbard, and a small part of the extremity of the blade. In the confusion consequent on the fire, the sword thus mutilated was mislaid, and for a long time it was supposed to be lost. In 1852, a committee was appointed by the Grand Lodge to make every exertion for its recovery, and at length, in the beginning of the year 1854, it was accidentally found by the Grand Tiler, in an outhouse on his premises, and was by him restored to the Grand Lodge in its mutilated condition. The lost piece of the blade was ingeniously replaced by a cutler in the city of Charleston, and being sent to New York, was returned with new hilt and velvet scabbard, and was used in its appropriate place during the centennial ceremonies of that year.

With such a history, and blended with such tradition of its origin, we need not feel surprised at the universal and keen feeling occasioned by its loss.

[CONTINUED IN OUR NEXT.]

COLUMBIA, S.C., SATURDAY, 8 APRIL 1865, VOL. 1, NO. 9.

XXX.

The morning of Saturday, the 18th of February, opened still with its horrors and terrors, though somewhat diminished in their intensity. A lady said to a Yankee officer at her house, somewhere about 4 that morning: "In the name of God, sir, when is this work of hell to be ended?" He replied: "You will hear the bugles at sunrise, when a guard will enter the town and withdraw these troops. It will then cease, and not before." Sure enough, with the bugle's sound and the entrance of fresh bodies of troops, there was an instantaneous arrest of incendiarism. You could see the rioters carried off in groups and squads, from the several precincts they had ravaged, and those which they still meditated to destroy. The tap of the drum, the sound of the signal cannon, could not have been more decisive in its effect, more prompt and complete. No farther fires were set, among private dwellings, after sunrise; and the flames only went up from a few places, where the fire had been last applied; and these were rapidly expiring. The best and most beautiful portion of Columbia lay in ruins. Never was ruin more complete; and the sun rose with a wan countenance, peering dimly through the dense vapors which seemed wholly to overspread the firmament. Very miserable was the spectacle. On every side ruins, and smoking masses of blackened walls, and towers of grim, ghastly chimneys, and between, in desolate groups, reclining on mattress, or bed, or earth, were wretched women and children, gazing vacantly on the site of a once blessed abode of home and innocence. Roving detachments of the enemy passed around and among them. There were those who looked and lingered nigh, with taunt and sarcasm. Others there were, in whom humanity did not seem wholly extinguished; and others again, to their credit, be it said, as wondrous exceptions from the usual characteristics of their comrades, who were truly sorrowful and sympathizing, who had labored for the safety of family and property, and who openly deplored the dreadful crime, which threatened the lives and honors of the one, and destroyed so ruthlessly the other.

XXXI.

But we have no time for description. The relentless fate was hurrying forward, and the destroyer had still as large a share of his assigned labors to execute. This day was devoted to the destruction of those buildings of a public character which had escaped the wreck of the city proper. The Saluda cotton manufactory, the property of Col. L. D. Childs, was burned by the enemy prior to their entry of the city and on their approach to it, the previous day. The several powder mills were destroyed on Saturday. The Arsenal buildings on Sunday, and it is understood that, in the attempt to haul away ammunition from the latter place, the enemy lost a large number of men, from an unlooked for explosion.[37] It is reported in one case that no less than forty men, with their officers—one entire company—were blown to pieces in one precinct, and half as many in another. But the facts can never be precisely ascertained, unless in the report of Yankee orderlies. The magnificent steam printing establishment of Evans and Cogswell —with the house assigned to their engravers, and another house, stored with stationery and book stock—perhaps the most complete establishment of the kind in the Confederacy—was destroyed on Saturday; their lithographic establishment, itself complete and singularly extensive, was burned in the general conflagration of Friday night. These were all private property, most of it isolated in situation, and deliberately fired. So, the fearful progress of incendiarism continued throughout Saturday and Sunday, nor did it wholly cease on Monday. The gas works—private property also—one of the greatest necessities of the people, was then deliberately destroyed; and it was with some difficulty that the incendiaries were persuaded to spare the water works. The cotton card manufactory of the State; the sword factory—a private interest; the stocking manufactory— private; the buildings at Fair Grounds, adjoining cemetery; the several railway depots; Alexander's foundry; the S. C. R. R. foundry and work shops—the Government armory, and other buildings of greater or less value, partly Government and party private property—all shared a common fate. Major Niernsee,[38] the State Architect, was a great loser, in his implements and valuable scientific and professional library. The new Capitol building, being unfinished, and not likely to be finished in many years—useless, accordingly to us—would have too greatly taxed the powder resources of the enemy to destroy it, and it was spared accordingly—only suffering from some petty assaults of malice. Here and there, a plinth fractured; here and there a Corinthian capital. The beautiful pillar of Tennessee marble was thus injured. So, at great pains-taking, the miserable wretches clambered up on ladders to reach and efface the exquisite scroll and ornamental work on the face of the building—disfiguring the beautiful chiseling which had wrought out the vine and acorn tracery on the several panels; and the bundles of fasces, on the Northern part, were fractured or broken away in parts. The statue of Washington[39] in bronze, cast in 1858, for the city of Charleston, from Houdon's original, in the rotunda at Richmond, received several bruises from brickbats, addressed to face and breast. A shell scratched his back, and the staff which he bore in his hand was broken off in the middle. But the bronze seems to have defied the destructives, and may be considered still perfect. The bust of Calhoun,[40] by Powers, was totally destroyed; so, also, was the ideal personification, by the sculptor Brown,[41] of the Genius of Liberty. A large collection of complete capitals, destined for the Capitol, and lying in the open square, were destroyed either by the heat of the contiguous fire, or by explosions of gun-powder introduced among them. Hereafter, such beautiful pieces of workmanship might be kept more safely and certainly, by being buried deeply in excavations of sand. The iron palmetto tree, that ingenious performance of Werner, of Charleston, dedicated as a monument to the Palmetto Regiment,[42] so renowned in the war with Mexico, suffered the loss of a number of its lower and larger branches; but these, we think, may be restored at comparatively little cost. The apartment in the base was torn open, having been wretched from its fastenings, but no other mischief seems to have been done to it. It was probably spared, as commemorating the deeds of those who had fought under their own flag, at a season when that flag was still held in some degree of honor, and was not wholly significant of shame and crime.

XXXII.

Something should be said in respect to the manner in which the negroes were treated by the enemy while in Columbia, and as regards the influences employed by which to beguile or take them from their owners. We have already adverted to the fact that there was a vast difference between the feelings and performances of the men from the West, and those coming, or directly emanating, from the Eastern States. The former were adverse to a connection with them; but few negroes were to be seen among these, and they were simply used as drudges, grooming horses, bearing burdens, humble of demeanor and rewarded with kicks, cuffs and curses, frequently without provocation. They despised and disliked the negro; openly professed their scorn or hatred, declared their unwillingness to have them as companions in arms, or in company at all. Several instances have been given us of their modes of repelling the association of the negro, usually with blow of the fist, butt of the musket, slash of the sword or prick of the bayonet. Sherman himself looked on these things indifferently, if we are to reason from a single fact afforded us by Mayor Goodwyn. This gentleman, while walking with the Yankee General, heard the report of a gun. Both heard it, and immediately proceeded to the spot. There they found a group of soldiers, with a stalwart young negro fellow lying dead before them on the street, the body yet warm and bleeding. Pushing it with his feet, Sherman said, in his quick, hasty manner, "What does this mean, boys?" The reply was sufficiently cool and careless. "The d—d black rascal gave us his impudence, and we shot him." "Well, bury him at once! Get him out of sight!" As they passed on, one of the party remarked, "Is that the way, General, you treat such a case?" "Oh!" said he, "we have no time for courts-martial and things of that sort!"

A lady showed us a coverlet, with huge holes burned in it, which she said had covered a sleeping negro woman, when the Yankees threw their torches into her bed, from which she was narrowly extricated with life.

Of the recklessness of these soldiers, especially when sharpened by cupidity, an instance is given where they thrust their bayonets into a bed, where they fancied money to be hidden, between two sleeping children—being, it is admitted, somewhat careful not to strike through the bodies of the children.

The treatment of the negroes in their houses was, in the larger proportion of cases, quite as brutal as that which was shown to the whites. They were robbed in like manner, frequently stripped of every article of clothing and provisions, and where the wigwam was not destroyed, it was effectually gutted. Few negroes, having a good hat, good pair of shoes, good overcoat, but were incontinently deprived of them, and roughly handled when they remonstrated. These acts, we believe, were mostly ascribed to Western men. They were repeatedly heard to say: "We are Western men, and don't want your d—d black faces among us." When addressing the negro, they frequently charged him with being the cause of the war. In speaking to the whites on this subject, especially to South Carolinians, the cause was ascribed to them. In more than one instance, we were told: "We are going to burn this d—d town. We've begun, and we'll go through. This thing began here, and we'll stack the houses and burn the town."

XXXIII.

A different role was assigned to, or self-assumed by, the Eastern men. They hob-a-nobbed with the negro; walked with him, and smoked and joked with him. Filled his ears with all sorts of blarney; lured him, not only with hopes of freedom, but all manner of license. They hovered about the premises of the citizens, seeking all occasion to converse with the negroes. They would elude the guards, slip into the kitchens, if the gates were open, or climb over the rear fences, and pour their subtle poison into the senses of all who would listen. No doubt they succeeded in beguiling many, since nothing is more easy than to seduce, with promises of prosperity, ease and affluence, the laboring classes of any people, white or black. To teach them that they are badly governed and suffering wrong, is the favorite method of demagogueism in all countries, and is that sort of influence which will always prevail with a people at once vain, sensual and ignorant. But, as far as we have been able to see and learn, a large proportion of the negroes were carried away forcibly. When the beguiler failed to seduce, he resorted to violence. The Yankees, in several cases which have been reported to us, pursued the slaves with the tenacity of blood-hounds; were at their elbows when they went forth, and hunted them up, at all hours, on the premises of the owner. Very frequent are the instances where the negro, thus hotly pursued, besought protection of his master or mistress, sometimes voluntarily seeking a hiding place along the swamps of the river; at other times, finding it under the bed of the owner; and not leaving these places of refuge till long after the enemy had departed. For fully a month after they had gone, the negroes, singly or in squads, were daily making their way back to Columbia, having escaped from the Yankees by dint of great perseverance and cunning, generally in wretched plight, half-starved and with little clothing. They represented the difficulties in the way of their escape to be very great, the Yankees placing them finally under guards at night, and that they could only succeed in flight at the peril of life or limb. Many of these were negroes of Columbia, but the larger proportion seemed to hail from Barnwell. They all sought passports to return to their owners and plantations.

XXXIV.

We should not overlook the ravage and destruction which marked the progress of the enemy in the immediate precincts of the city, though beyond its corporate boundaries. Within a few miles of Columbi[a], from two to five miles, it was girdled by beautiful country seats, such as those of the Hampton family— Millwood—a place famous of yore for its charm and elegance of society, its frank hospitality and the lavish bounty of its successive hosts.[43] The destruction of this family seat of opulence, and grace, and hospitality, will occasion sensation in European countries, no less than in our own, among those who have enjoyed its grateful privileges, as guests, in better days. This was destroyed by a gang of banditti, sent forth to forage—foraging, in Gen. Sherman's dictionary, being identical with burglary and arson. The beautiful country seats of Mr. Secretary Trenholm, of Dr John Wallace, Mrs. Thos. Starke, Col. Thomas Taylor, Capt. J. U. Adams, Mr. C. P. Pelham, Mill Creek,[44] as well as homestead—and many more—all shared the fate of Millwood—all were robbed and ruined, then given to the flames, and from these places were carried off all horses, mules, cattle and hogs, stock of every sort, and the provisions not carried off, were destroyed. In many cases, where mules and horses were not choice, they were shot down; and where the marauders abandoned their own beasts, in finding better, they almost invariably slew those which they left. But this was the common history. On all the farms and plantations, and along the road sides everywhere, for many a mile, horses, mules and cattle, strew the face of the country. Young *colts*, however fine the stock, had their throats cut. The same demonic spirit, prompted the destruction of every vehicle which the plunderers could not carry away. One informant tells us that in one pile he counted forty slain mules on the banks of the Saluda.

XXXV.

But there were other barbarities of more heinous character, reported of their proceedings in the more isolated farm settlements and country houses. Horrid narratives of rape are given which we dare not attempt to individualize. Individuals suspected of having concealed large sums of money, were hung up repeatedly, until, almost in the agonies of death and to escape the torture, they confessed where the deposit had been made. A family of the name of Fox, of Lexington, were treated with especial cruelty. The head of the family was hung up thrice by the neck till nearly dead, when he yielded $9,000 in specie to the robbers. Mr. Meetze, of the same district, is reported to have been robbed in like manner and by the same process; and one poor idiot—a crazy creature, mistaken for another party, was subjected, till nearly dead, to the same treatment. This mode of torture, from what we can learn, was frequently resorted to. Other parties were whipped; others buffeted or knocked down, and, indeed, every form of brutality seems to have been put in practice, whenever cupidity was sharpened into rage by denial or disappointment. But we sicken at the farther recital of these cruelties and horrors![45] The soul turns away with loathing from their contemplation. The heart bleeds, the mind, in despair, cries to the great Master of nations, with plea and prayer asking if there be no vengeance in the stores of heaven—no fiery bolts—to alight upon the heads of these fiends set free, and annihilate them with the sharpest and swiftest of dooms—such as justice and mercy and all the virtues must sanction with clapping of hands, even in the sacred abodes of eternity. Can it be that these reckless demons, mocking equally God and humanity, shall pursue with impunity their diabolical progress. Do they not march to retribution? Are they not cursed with such impediments, as will take courage out of their souls and strength out of their limbs? The spoils they have borne away from ten thousand desolated homes, must weigh equally upon their shoulders, their conscience and courage. Robbers are rarely brave men, and whatever might have existed in virtue of their cause, is forfeit by the processes which they have taken for its maintainance. Encountered by a determined enemy, stung by the sense of loss and suffering, intensified by the stings of such a record of violated homes, as is here written, they will surely quail before our sons. We look yet to behold the retribution, in its most terrible aspects, dogging their heels and tearing at their throats. The judgment of God on crimes of the foulest—the revenge of man, for deeds too terrible for humanity to contemplate —these, will arm our people, fighting *pro aris et focis*, with a power which they will face in vain—with a vengeance which shall teach them what they deserve, however little they may be prepared to endure.

COLUMBIA, S.C., MONDAY, 10 APRIL 1865, VOL. 1, No. 10.

Conflagration of Columbia

The reader will have seen that we have brought to a close our narrative of the most conspicuous of events, in the "capture, sack, and burning of the city of Columbia." We have been at great pains to make the statements ample, and to justify them by reference to the best authorities and witnesses to be found. We believe that the facts are substantially complete, and so, true in all respects. There are no doubt many omissions of interesting incidents, which, as they are reported to us, we may supply hereafter in a supplement. The incidents given are selected as typical of large groups of facts, representative anecdotes, uniform in their variety, and quite too numerous for separate consideration. But the very uniformity, amidst such a numerous collection, is in confirmation of the general authenticity of the whole; and we repeat the conviction that the narrative is wholly true withal, and to be relied on as a history.

We have seen, with some surprise, some attempts, in sundry quarters, to account for the destruction of Columbia, by ascribing it to accident, to the drunkenness of straggling parties, to our negroes, and, indeed, to any but the proper cause. It is evidently the design of these writers, without inquiring into the motives by which they were governed, to relieve the Yankee General and his army from the imputation. If it could be shown that one-half of Sherman's army were not actually engaged in firing the houses in twenty places at once, while the other half were not quiet spectators indifferently looking on, there might be some shrewdness in this suggestion. If it could be shown that the whiskey found its way out of stores and cellars, grappled with the innocent Yankees, and poured itself down their throats, then the Yankees are relieved of the responsibility. If it can be proved that the negroes were not terrified by the presence of these infu-riate enemies, in such large numbers, and did not, (as they almost invariably did,) on the night of the fire, skulk away into their cabins, lying quite low, and keep-ing as dark as possible; we might listen to this suggestion, and perhaps admit its plausibility. But why did the Yankees prevent the firemen from extinguishing the fire in its first outbreak, as they strove to do? Why did they cut the hose, as soon as it was brought into the streets? Why did they not assist in extinguishing the flames? Why, with 20,000 men encamped in the streets, did they suffer the stragglers to succeed in a work of such extensive and diabolical mischief? Why did they suffer the same wretches to break into the stores and drink the liquor wherever it was found? And what shall we say to the universal plundering, which was a part of the object attained through the means of fire? Why, above all, did they, with their guards massed at every corner, suffer the negroes to do this work? These questions answered, it will be seen that all these suggestions are sheer nonsense. To give them plausibility, we have been told, among other falsehoods, that General Sherman himself was burned out of his own selected quarters, no less than four times. This is simply false. He was burned out in no single instance. None of his Generals was burned out. The houses chosen for their abodes, were carefully selected, and the fire was studiously kept from approaching them in any single instance.

But we have pursued our narrative very imperfectly, if our array of facts be not such as conclusively to show that the destruction of the city was a deliberately designed thing, inflexibly fixed from the beginning, and its fate sufficiently well known to be conceived and comprehended by all the army.

Long before the enemy left Savannah, a lady inquired of one of the Yankee Generals in that city, whither she should retire—mentioning her preference of Columbia. His reply was significant—"Go anywhere but to Columbia." We have stated the conference between the lady superior of the Ursuline Convent, and a certain Major of the Yankees, who originally belonged to the press gang of Detroit. He warned her at 11 o'clock of Friday, "that she would need all the guard he had brought, *as Columbia was a doomed city.*"

A lady in one of our upper districts, expressing surprise at the treatment of Columbia in the nineteenth, or boasted century of civilization, was answered: "South Carolina has been long since the promised boon of Sherman's army." And it is well known that an order was issued to his troops before they crossed the river, giving them license to sack, plunder and destroy for the space of thirty-six hours.

Masonic brethren told others in the city, that this order had been issued, and that Columbia was destined to destruction. A sick Yankee soldier, who had been fed, nursed and kindly treated by a city lady, told her, on Friday morning, that the place would be destroyed that night; and the fact already glimpsed at, that the officers quartered themselves in the suburbs, and could not be found when the fire commenced, is sufficiently significant of the well understood design. The simultaneous breaking out of the fires, in the heart of the city, and in the suburbs in twenty places besides, should conclude all doubt. The attempt to lie it away, is as atrocious in its recklessness, as the deed which the falsehood is meant to palliate.

There are hundreds of witnesses who heard the explicit assertions to this effect from the common soldiery, and the detailed facts as already given, confirm their avowals. They were, as an army, completely in the hands of their officers. Never was discipline more complete—never authority more absolute.

1. Enough that Sherman's army was under perfect discipline.
2. That the fire was permitted, whether set by drunken stragglers or negroes, to go on, and Sherman's soldiers prevented, by their active opposition, all efforts of the firemen, while thousands looked on in perfect serenity, seeming totally indifferent to the event.
3. That hundreds of soldiers, quite sober, were seen in hundreds of cases busily engaged in setting the fire, well provided with all the implements and agencies, such as the most expert of city felons could conceive or devise.
4. That they treated with violence the citizens who strove to arrest the flames.
5. That, when entreated and exhorted by citizens to arrest the felons and prevent the catastrophe, at the very outset, the officers, in many cases, treated the applicants cavalierly, and gave no heed to its application.
6. That, during the raging of the flames, the act was justified by a reference to the course of South Carolina in originating the secession movement.
7. That the general officers themselves held aloof until near the close of the scene and of the night; were not to be found; and that Gen. Sherman's guard was not within the city; and yet no person could be ignorant of what was in progress. That Gen. Sherman knew what was going on, yet kept aloof and made no effort to arrest it, until daylight on Saturday, ought, of itself, be conclusive.
8. That, with his army under such admirable discipline, he could have arrested it at any moment; and that he did arrest it, when it pleased him to do so, even at the raising of a finger, at the tap of a drum, at the blast of a single trumpet.

But, what need of these and a thousand other suggestive reasons, to establish a charge which might be assumed from a survey of Sherman's general progress, from the moment when he entered South Carolina. Every subsequent step was taken in plunder and conflagration. The march of his army was a continued flame, the tread of his horse was devastation, the presence of his troops was significant of robbery and all brutalities. On what plea was the picturesque village of Barnwell destroyed? We had no army there for its defence; no issue of strength in its neighborhood had excited the passions of the combatants. Yet it was plundered—every house—and nearly all burned to the ground; and this, too, where the town was occupied by women and children only. So, too, the fate of Blackville, Graham, Bamberg, Buford's Bridge, Orangeburg, Lexington, &c.,

all hamlets of most modest character, where no resistance was offered—where no fighting took place—where there was no provocation of liquor even, and where the only exercise of heroism was as the expense of woman, infancy and feebleness. Such, too, was the fate of every farm-house—of six in seven, at least; those only being spared which held forth no temptation to lust and cupidity; or which were hurried by in the hopes of yet better prizes beyond. Surely, when such was the fate and treatment in all cases, there need be no effort now to show that an exception was to be made in favor of the State capital, where the offences charged upon South Carolina had been necessarily of the rankest character; and, when they had passed Columbia—greatly bemoaning the cruel fate which, under stragglers and whiskey-drinkers and negroes, had brought her to ruin, in spite of the tears and entreaties of their tender-hearted General—what were the offences of the villages of Allston, Pomaria, Winnsboro, Blackstocks, Society Hill and the towns of Camden and Cheraw? Thus weeping over the cruelty which so unhappily destroyed Columbia, was it that she should enjoy fellowship in woe and ashes, that they gave all these towns and villages to the flames, and laid waste all the plantations and farms between? But enough. If the conscience of any man be sufficiently flexible on this subject to coerce his understanding even into a momentary doubt, all argument will be wasted on him.

Our task has ended. Our narrative is drawn by an eye-witness of much of this terrible drama, and of many of the scenes which it includes; but the chief part has been drawn from the living mouths of a cloud of witnesses, male and female, the best people in Columbia.

Notes

1. In the 1865 revised pamphlet, Simms added chapter titles and deleted the word *Capture* in the title—the first of many changes employed to render his articles more suitable for a readership that would extend beyond the city of Columbia. While readers of the *Columbia Phoenix* may have felt as if their city had been captured, that perception was not based on fact. The undefended city was officially surrendered prior to the entry of Federal forces; thus, in reality, the defenseless city was not captured.

2. Two changes in section 1 demonstrate Simms's shift from newspaper editor with an immediate and local readership to author of a pamphlet intended for a wider readership. In the second sentence he replaced five words—"the cruel and malignant enemy"—with three words—"an invading army." The last sentence of section 1 ends with "as complete as possible," replacing the words "so that our sons may always remember, and the whole Christian world everywhere may read."

3. Gen. Joseph Eggleston Johnston (1807–1891).

4. Gen. John Bell Hood (1831–1879).

5. Gen. William Joseph Hardee (1815–1873).

6. "38,000" was later corrected to "33,000."

7. Thermopylae was the narrow pass in Greece protected—during the Persian invasion in 480 B.C.—by three hundred Spartans, who fought to the death of the last man.

8. "Partisan fighting" is a reference to the guerrilla tactics used in the South to defeat the British during the American War for Independence.

9. The last two sentences of this section were written before Simms learned of the events in Bentonville, North Carolina, on 19–21 March 1865 and before the Appomattox Campaign of 29 March–9 April 1865. Simms deleted the two sentences when preparing the 1865 pamphlet.

10. Although Simms deleted a significant amount of section 4, he retained in the 1865 pamphlet his observations about the treatment of the black population by the Federal soldiers, who left them to starve in what had been one of the richest states in America. The per capita income in South Carolina in 1860 made it the second wealthiest state in the country.

11. Gen. Wade Hampton (1818–1902), Gen. Joseph Wheeler (1836–1906), and Gen. Matthew Calbraith Butler (1836–1909).

12. Gen. Benjamin Franklin Cheatham (1820–1896) and Gen. Alexander Peter Stewart (1821–1908).

13. Gen. Evander McIvor Law (1836–1920). In the 1865 pamphlet, Simms added that General Law was "assisted by Mayor Goodwyn and Captains W. B. Stanley and John McKenzie." Thomas Jefferson Goodwyn was mayor of Columbia; William Stanley commanded the Palmetto Volunteer Fire Company while McKenzie commanded the Independent Volunteer Fire Company.

14. Andrew Gordon Magrath.

15. John McKenzie, Orlando B. Bates, and John Stork were the aldermen who accompanied Mayor Thomas Jefferson Goodwyn.

16. Captain William B. Platt of Gen. John A. Logan's staff and Col. George A. Stone of the 25th Iowa Infantry.

17. Gen. Oliver Otis Howard commanded the 15th Corps of Gen. John A. Logan and the 17th Corps of Gen. Francis P. Blair. In the 1865 pamphlet, Simms ended this paragraph with "The advance belonged to the 15th Corps." He deleted the reference to Howard as well as the last three sentences of the paragraph.

18. The mayor's letter of surrender and its request for protection of persons and property was sent by Stone to Sherman, who made no written acknowledgment of it. The assurances of safety that Stone made to the mayor were never committed to paper.

19. The list of property destroyed was removed from the body of the account and added at the end of the 1865 pamphlet. Typographical errors and misspelled names were corrected, and additional descriptions were supplied where needed. A review of the newspapers shows that Simms updated and corrected his list as necessary changes and new information were called to his attention by readers.

20. The dwelling was the French consul's house and the only building left standing after the fire destroyed the rest of Main Street, which was then two miles long.

21. Capt. Thomas R. Sharp was the quartermaster of transportation.

22. In the *Columbia Phoenix* of 28 March 1866, Simms noted he had been corrected by the Reverend L. P. O'Connell, post chaplain of the Catholic Church in Columbia, who informed him that General Sherman was not a Catholic, but his wife and daughters were Catholic converts, and his daughters were educated by the ladies of the Ursuline. The priest further asserted that he was not "knocked down" but was "severely handled." His watch was taken, and he was insulted during the violent tussle.

In his memoirs, published in 1875, Sherman acknowledged, "I received a note in pencil from the Lady Superioress of a convent or school, in Columbia, in which she claimed to have been a teacher in a convent in Brown County, Ohio, at the time my daughter Minnie was a pupil there, and therefore asking special protection. My recollection is, that I gave the note to my brother-in-law, Colonel Ewing, then inspector-general on my staff, with instructions to see this lady, and assure her that we contemplated no destruction of any private property in Columbia" (279ff.).

23. The Reverend Peter J. Shand.

24. Simms was fond of puns. The vulgar liquor is probably scotch whiskey. A Scotch verdict is an inconclusive judgment of pronouncement. *Sthale*, if pronounced "stale" and used as a verb, means to urinate. If pronounced "stall" and used as a verb, it means to delay or postpone. Interestingly, the word *stale* may represent a dialectal prununication of the word *steal*. Those familiar with Old English would consider *stale* and *steal* synonomous.

25. Mount Ararat is the traditional resting place of Noah's Ark.

26. Gen. O. O. Howard, known to many as the "Christian General," founded Howard University in Washington, D.C., and served as its president from 1869 to 1874. He had little patience with drunkenness or swearing and none for stealing. In a 20 February 1865 letter to General Blair, written from Rice Creek Springs, South Carolina, Howard calls Blair's attention "to the fact that some of our soldiers have been committing the most outrageous robberies of watches, jewelry, etc." He then provided examples of robberies known to the commissioned officers in charge and reported the violent assault of a lady being robbed of her gold watch. "These outrages," he declared, "must be stopped at all hazards, and the thieves and robbers who commit them be dealt with severely and summarily."

27. Edward Sill.

28. No rapes were officially reported. Omitting rape accounts is not surprising. Simms called such crimes "horrors which the historian dare not pursue." As Simms implied, the rapist was more likely to receive his punishment from a male member of the victim's family than from a law-enforcement official.

29. In the 1865 pamphlet "Mr. Melvin M. Cohen" was changed to "Mr. M.M.C." It is likely the change was made at Cohen's request, perhaps to protect his identity at a time when military occupation of the city could place his home and family at risk.

30. Empress was changed to Assembly Street in the 1865 pamphlet.

31. In the 1865 pamphlet "Mr. Jacob Cohen" was removed; the sentence refers to "Rev. Dr. O'Connell and others."

32. Cohen's name was again deleted in the 1865 pamphlet.

33. The Reverend Anthony Toomer Porter was an Episcopalian minister who had fled Charleston to find shelter for his wife and two children in the home of Dr. William Reynolds on Washington Street in Columbia.

34. This Colonel Ewell may have been Charles Ewing, then a colonel serving as inspector general on the staff of his brother-in-law. Sherman says in his memoirs that, in response to the mother superior's note, he sent Colonel Ewing to see her at the convent. It is possible Ewing made more than one visit.

35. Dr. Thompson is Surgeon Thomson, the public officer assigned to Second North Carolina Hospital, whose office was located in the South Carolina College chapel. Dr. Maximilian LaBorde, J. L. Reynolds, and W. J. Rivers all lived in campus housing.

36. Simms visited Masons of the North after the Confederate War and was able to secure assistance from them for the Masons of South Carolina.

37. The ammunition was being thrown into the river when a shell exploded. Flames ran along a trail of powder back to the wagons used for hauling and set off further explosions inside the still partially loaded wagons. Sherman said several wagons and teams of mules were lost in this accident, which killed sixteen men. In writing about the event Sherman's aide-de-camp G. W. Nichols said, "Several men were killed and twenty were wounded." In his 1865 pamphlet, Simms added this sentence: "The body of a Federal captain lay on the banks of the river for several days."

38. Maj. John Niernsee, engineer.

39. The statue of George Washington was one of six bronze copies of Jean Antoine Houdon's marble statue of Washington, which stands in the Capitol in Richmond. The W. J. Hubard Foundry of Richmond cast these copies of the French sculptor's statue for sale at ten thousand dollars apiece. Gov. R. F. W. Allston bought one in 1858 for South Carolina. It was paid for by legislative appropriations.

40. In *Marching through Georgia* (1890) F. Y. Hedley claimed the marble bust of John C. Calhoun "was made the target for inkstands and spittoons" while his fellow soldiers held a "mock senate" in the old senate chamber. The bust was by Hiram Powers.

41. Henry Kirke Brown also worked on a large pediment for the State House in Columbia from 1857 to 1861. It too was destroyed.

42. In *The Story of the Great March* (1865) Nichols discussed the monument and the names inscribed in brass letters at its base: "One of our stragglers, while attempting to detach some of these letters, was at first warned, and, not desisting, was seized and severely handled by the soldiers for the commission of what they regarded as a sacrilegious crime." Hedley wrote in *Marching through Georgia*, "This beautiful work of art was a palmetto tree of iron, so skillfully made that only the closest scrutiny revealed the fact that it was not a living tree."

43. Millwood was Maj. Gen. Wade Hampton's family home.

44. George A. Trenholm, Dr. John Wallace, Colonel Thomas Taylor, and Capt. James U. Adams. Mr. C. P. Pelham was owner of Mill Creek.

45. In preparing the 1865 pamphlet, Simms deleted everything after "But we sicken at the farther recital of these cruelties" until the last section, "Conflagration of Columbia," which he retitled "Conclusion."

INDEX

on railroad depot explosion, 54–55; on refugees in South Carolina, 50–51, 87–88; on residents' flight from fires, 87–88, 93–95, 98–99, 102; on residents' responses, 74–75, 85–88, 98–99, 100–101, 105; on robberies by Union soldiers, 61, 64–65, 73, 75–77, 84–87, 89–91, 108, 110; on ruins of city, 105–6; sample pages of, *following p. 63*; on saving of South Carolina College library, 96, 101–2; on Sherman's approach to Columbia, 52–53; on Sherman's march through the South, 48–53, 113–14; significance of, 2, 4, 30–31, 43; on surrender of Columbia, 55–56; text of, 47–114; on Union soldiers' charity, 86–87; on Union soldiers' disruption of funeral and cemeteries, 91; on Union soldiers' drunkenness, 73–74, 75, 95, 102, 111; on Union soldiers from West versus East, 63, 85, 107–9; on Union soldiers' plundering and pillage, 63, 74–77, 84–85; on Union soldiers' revelries, 74, 75; on Union troops' entry into Columbia, 61, 64; on Ursuline Convent and Academy, 62–63, 94–95, 112; on violence against residents, 76, 88, 89–90, 98, 101, 108, 110, 116n22; on women's experiences, 74–76, 85–91, 98–101, 105; on women's responses to Union soldiers, 85–88, 98–99, 100–101, 105; writing style of, 4, 26

Carlisle, J. H., 80
Carr, L., 68
Carroll, C., 59
Carroll, Chan., 72
Carroll, Charles R., 26
Cartwright, Mrs., 57
casualties, 28, 53, 54–55, 73–74, 106, 117n37
Cathcart, James, 56
Catholicism, 8, 10, 62–63, 94–96, 99, 116nn22–23
cattle. *See* animals
Cavis, A. T., 70

cemeteries, Union soldiers' disruption of, 91
Chambers, P. P., 56
Charleston: The Place and the People (Ravenel), 23
Charleston City Gazette, 15, 27
Charleston Mercury, 15
Charleston, S.C.: W. G. Simms's birth in, 21; businesses in, 22; and Civil War, 14, 52, 86, 117n33; Fraser on, 10; Masonic lodges in, 103; and Revolutionary War, 22–23, 33; schools in, 10, 11; Secession Convention in, 20; Simms family in, 22; wealth of, 52; yellow fever in, 88
Charlotte Railroad, 79
Cheatham, Benjamin Franklin, 53, 115n12
Cheraw, S.C., 114
Cherokees, 24
Chesnut, James, 29
Chesnut, Mary Boykin, 29, 30
Cheves, Langdon, 9
children, 92, 93, 100, 108
Childs, L. D., 56, 106
Chisolm, John Julian, 29
Chrietzberg, J., 60
churches, 10, 62, 72, 79, 83, 84, 93–94, 116n22
Citadel, 10, 11
Civil, A., 56
Civil War: burning of Woodlands Plantation during, 28–29; casualties of, 28, 53, 54–55, 73–74, 106, 117n37; Charleston during, 14, 52, 86, 117n33; and Columbia before its destruction, 13–14, 29–31, 50–52; Confederate artillery during, 49–50; Faulkner on, 43; hospitals for wounded during, 13, 96, 102, 117n35; manufacturing facilities in Columbia during, 13, 51; printing operations for Confederacy during, 13; refugees in South Carolina during, 50–51, 87–88; removal of Johnston as commander of Confederate armies in Georgia, 47–48, 49; Sherman's march through the South during, 48–53, 113–14; Simms family in Columbia during, 28–29; women's desire

violence: against blacks, 107–8; against Columbia residents, 76, 88, 89–90, 98, 101, 108, 116n22; in farm settlements and country houses, 110

Volger, C., 67

Volger, Madame, 67

Waddell, Samuel, 70, 80

Wade, Thomas H., 72

Wadlow, D., 68

Wagner, S. J., 53

Walker, J. C., 66–67, 73

Walker, Joseph, 68

Walker, Mrs., 71

Walker, W. W., 67, 80

Wallace, John, 65, 109, 118n44

Walsh, P., 68

Walter, W. T., 59

Walter, Wm., 80

Wannamaker, Rev. T. E., 81

War for American Independence. *See* Revolutionary War

War of 1812, 22, 24

war poetry, 25–26

Ward, Miss S., 71

Washington, George, 7, 18; statue of, 107, 117n39

Washington, D.C., 6, 7

Washington Irving and His Literary Friends at Sunnyside (Schussele), 17–18

Washington Monument, 7

water supply, 5, 14

Watkins, Dr., 82

Watson, William, 60

Waud, William, *following p. 63*

Wearn, Richard, *following p. 63*, 67, 70, 71

Wells, C., 61, 82

Wells, James L., 81

West, William Edward, 16

Wheeler, Joseph, 52, 55, 61, 115n11

When the World Ended (LeConte), 6, 31–32

Whilden, Mrs. M., 80

White House (Washington, D.C.), 6

Wier, Mrs., 35

Wigwam and the Cabin . . . First Series, The (Simms), 15

William IV, King of England, 19

Williams, W., 82

Willis, Nathaniel Parker, 17

Wilson, Hugh, 35

Wimsatt, Mary Ann, 40–41

wine industry, 11–12

Winnsboro, S.C., 114

Winnstock, N., 69

women: in Columbia during Civil War, 29, 30, 52, 54; and desire for news, 14; during destruction of Columbia, 74–76, 85–91, 98–101, 105; illness of, during destruction of Columbia, 91; in labor during destruction of Columbia, 90–91, 93; murder of, 90; rape of, 89–90, 110, 116n29; writings by, on destruction of Columbia, 14

Woodlands Plantation, 19–21, 28–29, 38, 39

Woolley, Deborah K., 5–6

Wright, G. W., 78

Wright, Henry, 12–13

Yankee Doodle, 16

yellow fever, 88

Young, Captain, 101

Zealy, J. T., 73

Zealy, Mr., 60

Zernow, Mrs., 59

Zotor, V., 16